FOR MY MOM
AND
LOLA DELIA

PAINTING YOUR PATH

CLARISSA CASTILLO-RAMSEY

Library of Congress Control Number: 2020906633

The information in this book is written for inspirational purposes and not meant for individual advice.

Printed in the United States of America

ISBN 978-1-7344530-0-3

CONTENTS

Interviews

Why This Book, Why Now?

This book is about reinvention and defining your life on your terms.

It started out as a series of conversations with other dynamic and evolved women in my life as I found myself asking, "What's next?" "Am I satisfied with where I am at now in life?" These are questions every person asks at one, or two or many times in their life—perhaps after they've hit a milestone and are ready to set a new one. Many women come to a realization they were living more for other people and not for themselves. Maybe they awaken to the fact that they have spent too much time climbing a ladder that they no longer want to climb.

I'm a researcher at heart, and when I'm curious about a topic, I explore it. Before I became a coach, I explored the topic in my dissertation. I interviewed executives in organizations to learn how they leverage coaching in their companies. I also went through a coaching program at CTI, The Coaches Training Institute. Like any good organizational psychologist, I ask questions; I connect with people I can learn from; I seek different perspectives. I want to discover best practices so I can apply them.

I thought I could understand my own unique position in life better from talking with others. As I spoke with other women in my social sphere who were feeling the same way, I found that these conversations were becoming a passion project.

While I was preparing to write this book, I found several books about the lives of famous women. They were very inspiring, but I knew that there were more stories to be told. There are so many women out there being courageous, carving new paths for themselves. Why not share their stories too? I believe they could inspire someone who is on the cusp of doing something extraordinary.

"I love my company, I love what I do, I love my partners, I love my bands, and I'm still completely identifying myself as a band manager and a mother, but what about Deb. Who's Deb?"

"What's my second or third or fourth or fifth act going to be?"

"I don't want to be around these people anymore. Everyone else seemed so into it, but all I could think was 'This is my nightmare!'"

"I thought, 'Oh, this is definitely not the life I want for myself!'"

These are a few pieces of the conversations I had with different women about their life paths.

And so, I decided to compile them into a series. I wanted to write about women's journeys through life—in particular after 40—as a way to organize my own questions and help me work through my own doubts and fears. Although I've reinvented myself throughout my life and immersed myself in different careers, for some reason this wondering was different. As I have grown older and wiser while navigating a number of career pivots, I am really getting present to the fact that life is short; it's best to live our best lives now.

This book is a compilation of 21 interviews I conducted between 2018 and 2019. Some of these women were former co-workers, people I knew who were moving on to different careers or branching out on their own. I also put a request out on social media to different Facebook groups such as Cathy Heller's "Don't Keep Your Day Job" and Jenna Kutcher's "Goal Digger," asking if there were any women out there over 40 who were making major shifts in their lives. Several women "raised their hands" to talk with me. Then I asked the women interviewed if they knew any women in similar circumstances who I could potentially speak with. That's how this book took shape.

While the women share their personal histories, the discussion about their present situation is simply a snapshot in time. By the time this book is published, I'm sure there will be much more to their stories! These women are continuing to do great things in their lives, making transformations and evolving while touching the lives of others.

With each interview, I tapped into my background as an artist to create a piece of artwork with their favorite color and quote. I wanted to celebrate this special group of women somehow. Nearly everyone I know has a favorite color and a favorite saying which gives them energy. I made each person a piece of art unique to them. I've sent each interviewee their painting as a thank-you for sharing their journey. I have also included their social media information in case you, dear reader, would like to connect with any of them.

After the interviews, you'll find a short chapter on my story and journey as well as insights from my experiences. I did not intend to share my story, but as I was going through this process, a few of the women I interviewed asked me: What about you?

My hope is that this book inspires at least one woman to take action on a dream they have been putting off for fear that "it's too late." I love quotes, and one that came to mind when I wrote this book was "Be bold enough to use your voice, brave enough to listen to your heart, and strong enough to live the life you have always imagined." - Anonymous

Life is short. Whether there is a career or hobby you've always wanted to pursue or a life experience you've been putting off, the time is now. May you be inspired to take action on whatever it is you've been wanting to do. ∎

ENDORSEMENTS

I've been in the professional workforce for 25 years and have had only two colleagues that I consider to be great and intuitive leaders. The better of those two is Clarissa Castillo-Ramsey.

Her consistency and desire to grow her team of employees leaves them in a position to know…how she will guide them to success and, in the end, let them embrace that success as their own. Clarissa is an outstanding example of compassionate leadership combined with a firm hand on the controls that drive success for the organization.

Sara Mast, Manager, Talent Development

Clarissa is an insightful, mindful and experienced life coach. She gave me advice, guidance and the motivation that I was lacking. Through her supportive results-based coaching, I was able to visualize my goals and create a blueprint for my life.

Joanna Revel, Creative Director/Owner, Blue Violet Boutique and Captured Corners Photography

Her encouraging words, constant communication, and creative methods have been vital to improving my overall development. Clarissa is a skilled facilitator and trusted mentor, with a depth and breadth of personal experience that gives her the ability to relate to people from all walks of life. Knowing her has enriched me as a whole.

Katherine Novales, Regional Manager

Clarissa is an inspirational member of any group. Clarissa is an active listener and utilizes her creative skill set in seeking solutions to intricate organizational issues and processes.

Phil Patent, Founder, P2 Consulting

Clarissa has a magnificent way of identifying with people of all backgrounds, personalities and work/management styles. She is diplomatic and passionate, and her boundless creativity offers a great deal of perspective to any project. I always walked away from our interactions having learned something.

Ellen Belot Roggemann, Brand and Marketing Executive

Clarissa sees me. She helps me to grow and believe in myself, and even when I might not believe I can do it, she assures me I can. She backs up her beliefs with action—ways in which I can begin to take that leap into the unknown. I'm so grateful to have her in my life... And she doesn't let you off the hook, in a good way.

Joan Spinelli, Renaissance Woman

IF YOU STAY AT THE TABLE LONG ENOUGH, THE CHIPS COME TO YOU.

-HENRY WINKLER

ANNA BRAFF

Tell me a little bit about you as a kid. What was it like growing up for you?

My life was complicated as a child. My parents divorced when I was two, and I lived with my mother and sister. Following the divorce, my mother packed us up, and we lived in Georgia with my grandparents, which I actually loved. They had horses, land and lots of room in which to nurture our imaginations. We played in our toy room, played outside all the time, rode horses and so much more. After both my grandparents passed away, my mom—who had no brothers, sisters or any family in Georgia—wanted to move to Connecticut, where she had distant relatives. We were not very close to them. In a lot of ways, we felt very excluded from our distant relatives, but my mom needed a support system. My mom is an amazing person who would do anything for her kids and grandkids. She always encouraged our artsy sides, as well as our education, and wanted to be supportive in the best ways she could be. We lived in a small town in Connecticut until I moved to New York City for college. I followed my sister to college at New York University.

Favorite hobbies?

I LOVE traveling more than anything. I still do. Unfortunately, I don't get much of a chance to travel like I used to. I am excited that my husband, children and I will be going to Hawaii for our first real family vacation—usually, we travel more locally with the kids. I hope to do more traveling in the coming years.

What did you want to be when you grew up?

While I was growing up, it changed all the time. I loved the arts; I loved acting; I thought I wanted to be a model. I also thought I wanted to be an astronaut—I had a Barbie with a pink shiny spacesuit. I always knew I wanted to be something important. I never thought, "I want to be an entrepreneur!"

Can you share a little bit about your career path? What did that look like?

I studied acting in college and even pursued it after school. Film is a really tough industry. It is kind of disappointing and heartbreaking, what with all the rejection. I think people prey on dreamers too much in that field, and I was wasting my talents on something that felt shallow and sad.

I decided I wanted a stable career where I wouldn't have to rely on other people, so I thought law was it. It was an intellectual challenge, but it was not the right fit for my personality. I finished law school, passed the bar the first time I took it, practiced briefly…and then I got married and had a family. I hated being away from my children; I knew I had to spend more time with them.

Having my children really helped me get out of that situation I didn't like in law. It created space and helped me let go of the fear of not working for a while to think about what I enjoyed. My husband was also supportive of me pursuing my passion. He just wanted me to be happy.

Around the time my second child was a few months old, we planned a naming ceremony for him. I put in more effort to create this beautiful party for him than I did with my own wedding. After that, I knew I wanted to do something with events and props. I did not want to part with the beautiful items I had collected.

A friend who attended the party approached me with the idea to start a small business. We tried it, but we had very different ideas and parted ways eventually. I continued on with the company, made a small pivot, and rebranded as a vintage and specialty rentals company and design house—basically a niche prop house. (https://provenancerentals.com). We curate a one-of-a-kind collection to rent out furniture and props for events, photo shoots, television shows, weddings and much more. Like many things, it started off as a side hustle and expanded. Design was something I always loved and was good at.

How do you balance it all?

I don't know, since I still am learning how to balance. I do feel that as they are getting a little older (4 and 6), they are more independent—and in school at least part time! I sometimes take my kids with me to design meetings, and they have even been with me to set up weddings—but I try to avoid that unless necessary. In a way, though, they get an education in being an entrepreneur. As Oscar Wilde said, "Experience is the best teacher."

What's one life experience that has shaped your character?

I am sure the biggest thing is my parents' divorce and growing up with my single mother. Everything that happens in those first five years shapes your whole life.

What is the best advice you've received?

Charge your worth! And take steps to action rather than perseverating over things.

And the best book you've read?

I know it seems crazy, but *In Cold Blood* by Truman Capote is an amazing book. The detail in the writing is perfect. Even if the story is dark, you can really see the writer's genius at work.

What's the lesson you've had to learn over and over?

Learning to say no and stick to it. "No" is such an important word. It is actually quite positive, since to me, it signals boundaries and self-care.

What message would you like to share with our readers who might be on the fence about making a change in careers/vocation a little later in life?

Life is short. Many people talk about their regrets at the end of life; I don't want to be one of them. I would rather try and fail than not try at all. ∎

 @provenancerentals    @provenancerents

CLAUDIA SVIHRAN

Tell me a little bit about yourself as a child. What was growing up like for you?

My mom was 39 when she had me. I am an only child. My parents separated when I was 7. However, they remained close, even though they no longer lived under the same roof. I remember summer trips, weekends and holidays together. I did not ever feel traumatized by their divorce. I don't recall my childhood as a cheerful, happy one, but I had everything a child could want. I was raised with attention and care. Being an only child, I played alone a lot and discovered books in my teens, which took me to different worlds.

I fantasized about a more sophisticated and very different life. I guess it is only *normale*, as Italians say. My generation didn't have access to such things and fun experiences as today's kids, so we were constantly daydreaming about something more awesome than our rather simple and gray reality. Books, foreign cultures, design, fine art, music, history and even religion remained a very strong part of my life and shaping my identity.

Then I became a teenager and discovered boys! They found me pretty, and I started flirting. Like many adolescent girls, my interests shifted to dating. However, I remained rather self-conscious because I endured years of bullying from girls in class throughout primary school and high school. I was bullied because girls thought I was ugly and skinny–not worthy of boys' attention. I sort of agreed with them, but I ended up getting attention from the boys. To me, boys were an escape from my rather plain life. All my high school boyfriends seemed to have a more glorious life than I did, so my curiosity drove me to them.

What were your favorite hobbies? Did you know what you wanted to be when you grew up?

Reading about history and everything I could find about the Aztecs, Olmecs, Toltecs and the Inca Empire! I loved to draw–mostly interior design. My father was an architect, and he encouraged me to become an architect and interior designer. I went to an architectural high school and graduated as an architect technician. To my father's deepest regret, I didn't continue my studies to become an architect-engineer, and instead chose the world of advertising. I studied international marketing in Budapest and marketing management in Sydney.

Can you share a little bit about your career path? What did that look like?

My first workplace was at an advertising agency. I was still attending the university and started there as an "all-arounder." Basically, that meant I was rotating through different jobs. During my three years there, I became an assistant and later on, a manager. Over the past 25 years, I have never strayed away from the advertising industry.

I worked at several multinational companies, such as DDB, Ogilvy, Young & Rubicam, McCann, and Havas. I never ventured to the client side, as I always wanted to stay close to the creative fire, where ideas are born and manifested in great copy and images. As I advanced in my career, I loved the strategic aspects of my job: how a brand is driven to perform better in all measures. In the last eight to 10 years, my responsibilities have shifted to team leadership, business development and operational duties.

As the market is small in Hungary, there is less room for local creative planning and development. The assignments got less and less exciting. Despite the huge transformation that digital solutions brought to the advertising industry, the tasks remained very repetitious and brainless. I felt like I had already seen it all. A slow burnout started to take place. Money kept me there, as did the fact that I had no clue what else I would do. I mean, I had many ideas of what I would love to do with my days and nights; unfortunately, none of them were ways to make a living.

Where are you up to now?

My boredom with the industry and the state of my demotivation climaxed a few months ago. I thought, if I have to look at another meaningless online campaign, or look into the dull, thoughtless eyes of a mediocre client, or convince the management about a better pricing strategy that they will veto one day and demand additional profit the next, I will scream. So, when I had the last straw, during a project at my latest workplace, I stood up and resigned. I resigned not only from that place but from the whole industry. Of course, it had been growing in me gradually for a decade now, but it finally became reality.

I had a business idea taking shape in my head. Having full emotional and financial support from my spouse, I felt good about my decision. I am interested in culture and art, and in helping our society and the world to become more livable. I am interested in a purpose! Creating mediocre, dull ads is not what I can call a purpose.

I started working for Hungary's biggest auction house as the personal assistant of the owner. He is a true icon in the Hungarian art scene, dedicating himself to the preservation of 19th and early 20th-century Hungarian paintings. I have learned a lot and been totally enchanted by the whole scene. This is definitely something with which I would like to remain engaged! I am now organizing an independent exhibition for a private collector that will open in the fall of 2020.

During this break from my day job, I have accomplished a lot that matters to me on a personal level: my son's development and advancement; we have reinvested in a property for financial security; we've gotten more involved in the art industry that had long intrigued me. The next objectives are: getting more involved in this scene—either via work or study—and finding the opportunity to start up in this or a closely related area with my own small business.

What's a life experience that has shaped your character?

Several experiences. Bullying, for sure. It made me doubt myself for many, many years. I also got divorced, which was less painful, as it was mutual—but the fear of being alone with all the duties of a working mom at the age of 38 paralyzed me. My self-consciousness—the feeling of not being good enough—is hardly noticeable now, as I built myself up and strengthened my esteem, but it comes up every now and again, especially in new life situations. However, all in all, I consider myself very fortunate. I have had a very colorful and rich life so far with no major dramas, no big emotional or financial challenges or health issues. The thread of the past 30 years is an ongoing life experience that has shaped me into a positive, happy and life-loving person, who finally came to dare to change her career.

I changed my place of residence at a young age, went to live in Australia for four years. I changed my family status many times, by giving birth to my son, separating from his father, falling in love again, more truly and deeply than ever before. I've moved in with my boyfriend and am joining my life and my son's life with his.

And finally, I am changing my career path. It seems to be the least organic, most difficult transition. Perhaps I am older and hence more afraid, more conscious. Perhaps it is really about stepping out of my comfort zone, as the other things just happened to me, but with the career transition, it was a decision I initiated.

A book that has made an impact on you and why?

Dune: It showed me that when things reach the edge they overflow, and then everything goes back to zero and starts anew.

The Secret: Its technique seemed to work for me in big life matters—getting pregnant or saving my relationship.

Ministry of Utmost Happiness: It showed me how cruel the world is and how fragile good moments are.

What's a lesson you've had to learn over and over?

To let things go. Take things easier. Stop controlling.

What, if anything, keeps you up at night?

I sleep well, but I occasionally toss and turn over financial instability, fear of not having enough quality time with my son, securing my future and retirement.

What message would you like to give to our readers who are on the fence about trying a different career or embarking on a new venture while in their 40s and beyond?

Don't be afraid to act, but prepare well before making any big changes. Always have a security "plan B." Don't burn all the bridges, as at this age, responsibility for other's lives that are intertwined with yours is unavoidable. Don't stick to anything that doesn't make you happy! There is still a lot of life to live, don't live it miserably! Dare now because you may not be able to later. As you get older, it will get harder to change or to take up new challenges. You are still full of energy and potential, so do it now! Halfway down the road, you can look back with all the experience you have gained to evaluate what bags you do not need to carry on anymore and what are the destinations you haven't yet been but heard about and would love to reach. ∎

messenger: Claudia Svihran   email: csvihran@yahoo.com.au

I can resist EVERYTHING except TEMPTATION — OSCAR WILDE

DEB KLEIN

Tell me a little bit about the early years.

I moved all over the place as a child and went to three high schools. I ended up in Boston, going to Northeastern. It was too big of a school. I thought I wanted to be an aerospace engineer, but really, I was just fascinated with reading science fiction. I ended up in the business school at Northeastern, and I was just really unhappy. I dropped out, moved out of the dorms, and moved back home. I took a summer class at Emerson College in radio production. I had always loved music. I fell in love with it, so that's where I ended up. This was back in the old days of radio when you could play whatever you wanted, and I was cutting tape and editing and producing radio programs.

I became the program director of my college station, WERS. I graduated with honors cum laude with a plan: I was gonna be a DJ and the program director of a radio station. I thought I had it all figured out.

What did your early career look like?

I got a DJ gig right after I graduated from college. I was also working at a record store. The radio station gig was a real eye-opener for me of what was going on in the music industry. There was real #MeToo kind of stuff happening. Not to me personally, because I would tell people to F off. I was promised a music director position at the station, and the program director was pursuing me and making promises, and it turned out there was not even a job position at all.

It was just very male, sexist and gross. They told you what to say and what to play; and it wasn't anything like the utopia of college radio. I was hanging out with a lot of people in local rock bands because I was working at the record store. I ended up having dinner with this entertainment lawyer and a band and listening to this guy talk about the contract. I was like, "I'm smarter than him. I could do this."

That's when I decided to go to law school. It was kind of almost like, "Oh, let's just see if I can get in." I didn't study or prep before I took the LSAT, and I got a great score. I'll never forget, right before I took the LSAT, I went and saw the Butthole Surfers play, and then I aced it the next day.

Where did law school take you?

I was going to be an entertainment lawyer, specifically for music. I wanted to help musicians by using my brain and helping to make the world a better place through music. I saw a lot of musicians struggling. Especially in that time: the '80s. Musicians kind of took the long road, right? And when they were finally successful, the people that were left behind saw them as sellouts. Like when Nirvana got signed.

When I graduated from law school, I couldn't find a job as a lawyer. "Oh, shit. What do I do now?" I did get a job right before I graduated at this record label called Taang! Records. It was a local Boston record label that put out all kinds of punk rock bands. They also had bands like the Lemonheads and The Mighty Mighty Bosstones, these bands that were taking off.

I'd be there all day, working away. The owner was having a hard time with his business. I basically turned his business around. We had holds, we had creditors and also people that owed us money. I cleaned it up. Within three years, I probably put out 50 albums during that time for him. It was fun, and I was using my brain to help musicians and get them paid. The more I was working for the label, the more I thought I really wanted to be on the side of the artist, not the label. There was a sentiment out there that the label would just F you. That's how it was back then.

So what was next for you?

I was also practicing law on the side. I'd have indie label clients. They were artists that needed help with a contract. I did a lot of indie label negotiations for bands. I actually represented Elliott Smith when he was in this band called Heatmiser, which was before he had a solo career.

I was the lawyer for Morphine. Mark Sandman, the lead singer, was a really good friend of mine. He asked me to do his record deal. I did the deal for him, and afterward he said, "Well, I need a manager. Will you be my manager?" I had never officially managed a band before, and I had this feeling that

Mama

I don't think

I know

everything.

—EMMA, age 3

this band was gonna blow up, and I would be part of that, so I managed the band. They played all over Boston—people loved them.

I said, "I can't quit my job. How am I gonna get paid?" Mark said, "Well, you get paid 10%." I knew that wouldn't work, I had law school loans to pay off. He agreed to 15%. Within six months of starting to manage Morphine, they took off, and I was able to quit Taang! and support myself. I started my own company at the age of 26. I managed Morphine for their entire career. I decided to move to LA. Finally, after eight years of managing Morphine, Mark was ready to let me spread my wings. He had originally wanted my full focus and attention, which is why the band was so successful. I hadn't been juggling a lot of things; I had just been focused on them.

What happened post-Morphine?

My entire identity at that time was my work and what I was doing. I loved it. I was successful. I had realized my purpose. I was helping artists make money, make careers, using my brain, feeling good about it, all that. I stopped practicing law because I was managing. I was managing Sebadoh and Folk Implosion to name a few. Mark's death and the end of Morphine was a very difficult time for me because my identity was very tied up in that community.

Post-Morphine, I was about 34 years old, and I got pregnant. I hadn't been really planning on that. I was in the process of moving; a lot was going on. I had lots of swirling thoughts like, "Oh, my gosh. This is amazing!" or "I never thought I was gonna have a child," and "I really want this baby. I really want this child." I felt like it was something that was gonna change my life radically. I had not planned for it in any way, shape or form, but I had been told that I was going to meet the love of my life when I was 35, and it turned out to be my kid.

What happened next?

While I was pregnant, I did all kinds of weird jobs. I worked at Harvard Business School, and I was a scribe for the negotiations class for their MBA program, which was really interesting. I thought: I'm getting paid while I'm learning something. Then I also started a company called Little Cooks, which was almost like a franchise, and I did kids' birthday parties, cooking-themed parties. I just wanted to see what it was like to be around kids of all ages… "I gotta see what this kid thing's all about." I taught music industry at Northeastern University, which was a way of coming back around full circle.

How exciting! What happened with all the music managing?

Well, I had some money to live on. It wasn't a lot of money, but it was something. I kept a toe in the music world by teaching. That was short-lived though. I'm a doer. I'm not gonna sit there and talk about it. It was interesting to be a mentor: seeing these younger people and kind of schooling them. The Harvard thing—I just needed to make some money. I wanted some income. At seven months pregnant, I knew I needed to make money. I didn't want to use up all my savings. There was just something telling me that I really needed to move to Los Angeles.

A friend set me up with some meetings in LA. It must've been after I had Emma, my daughter. She was 5 or 6 months old, and her dad was still kind of around. I came out to California; I did a bunch of meetings. And basically, everyone told me, "Just move out here. You'll find something. You just need to be here."

I had been introduced and set up, but still, it took forever. I met with so many people. People you've probably heard of. I sold my condo, put everything in a moving van, and completely started over at the age of 35. No job, no nothing, I moved me and my 1-year-old from Boston to LA. I was in my cousin's apartment for like a week and then I found the house that I'm in now. I settled in LA. I'm not leaving.

A new adventure. How were the early LA days?

I literally had to start all over again after I had run a very successful business—and with a baby. I knew it would be better for me to work for somebody else and learn from other people in order to get bigger in the industry. At that point, I had only done indie label bands. Even though I signed Morphine to a major label, it was still like they had been an indie band.

I was with Spivak Sobol Entertainment. They gave me free office space. I found day care for my child. They said, "Just come in here, and we'll give you free office space if you do our legal agreements for our management contracts. Then when the right act comes along to manage, we'll work something out." Going into an office—I'd never done that before. Like never. I had always worked from my house. I had my own office at home—it was a big loft space back in Boston, and it was separate from where I lived. They were like, "Here's Vanessa Carlton. You can manage her." She was a platinum artist. She was huge. "Here's Eve 6, you can manage them. Do the day-to-day on Eve 6." Then they asked me what kind of bands I like and who I'd want to sign. I signed Yellowcard, and they blew up, went platinum. I took them from zero to platinum, pretty much. Then I found this band Flyleaf, and I took them from zero to platinum.

Then, SSE was bought out by a bigger company. I was at that firm for eight years, managing very big bands. I was managing Smashing Pumpkins and also running a record label again because at The Firm they had started a label. I got experience in running an independent record label. I knew how to do profit loss and a budget for an album.

We managed artists from Kelly Clarkson to Korn and everybody in between, including Backstreet Boys, Audioslave, Enrique Iglesias, Linkin Park. We had the biggest bands ever. I went from completely indie to working for this huge company with over a hundred people, working with some of the biggest bands in the world, touring the world. I was learning everything that I needed to learn that I hadn't learned from doing it on my own or from Mark Sandman.

And then, at some point, I started to hate it. I was beginning to feel like it wasn't me. It was still very male-dominated. Work was intense, and you were expected to be available 24/7. I was in the golden handcuffs. I had an employment agreement, and after I had been there for five years, I was making more money than I had ever made. It was salaried, and it was guaranteed, but they worked you.

I also needed to focus on the health of my daughter, Emma. I didn't want to quit, because then I would lose the employment agreement. I was doing my job, and I was not happy. I was stressed out. I was overweight due to health issues, with no time to take care of myself because I was so busy taking care of everyone else. So, the blessed day came, and I was asked to leave.

So then what, Deb?

That night, after maybe five minutes of tears, I went out and bought an iPhone and said, "I'm gonna start my own management company again." My daughter was incredible. She said, "That's a great idea. You should totally do that. You can do that." She's very encouraging, "I know you can do that."

I had my own company for eight years before I worked for somebody else. I never wanted to have another boss, ever again. I made a vow, and so, six years ago, I started my own management company. I called it Cosmic MGMT (this was a nod to a label I started years ago called Cosmic Records). I started over again from scratch for the third time, but this time, with all this experience from a very high level. I knew I could do it my way instead of their way, which was very aggressive. I'm going to do it intelligently, the way I've done it before. I was able to wait for the right opportunities and sign bigger bands, instead of just taking risks and signing a bunch of smaller bands.

Then a couple of friends of mine told me about Primary Wave. They're really interested in doing joint ventures. The CEO, Larry Mestel, really wanted a female executive at a high level to partner up with. I was like, "Hmm, that could be interesting." I did a joint venture with them five years ago, a year after I started my own company. I still have my own company, and I don't have a boss, but I have partners.

It has enabled me to have a platform to go out and sign bigger bands. I was at a lunch meeting, and I called Larry and asked: "Do we want to manage Melissa Etheridge?" "Yes, we want to manage Melissa Etheridge." So I was like, "OK, great. Let's go get her."

We got her. "Larry, do we want to manage Cypress Hill?" He's like, "Yes, we want to manage Cypress Hill." I was like, "OK, let's go get them." We got them. Lots of people who are established, looking for new energy, a different approach or a fresh approach. I signed Chris Robinson from the Black Crowes. He's got an amazing band called The Chris Robinson Brotherhood. I signed the Plain White T's after they got dropped from a Hollywood major record label and kind of restarted and rebooted their career. I haven't pivoted exactly, but it's been almost like having to rebuild or start over three times.

So, what's on the horizon for you?

I love my company; I love what I do; I love my partners; I love my bands; and I'm still completely identifying myself as a band manager and a mother— but what about Deb? Who's Deb? What's my second, or third, or fourth or fifth act going to be? There were two things that really spoke to me. One of them is cannabis. I'm still in the process of figuring out this piece, but it's a very natural fit with all my clients. I'm going to see where this takes me, and of course, it'll be another source of revenue. My intention is to keep on managing bands and bring an ancillary source of income for them, and to see if I want to do more in that area myself. I've also been doing some institutional investing, as an angel investor, and managing a group of women. We pooled our money together to invest in funds that we couldn't on our own. So, we're doing some financial stuff that's also very interesting to me. Not that I would do that for a living, but hopefully I can make enough money to live off of it.

The other thing I did last year was to get certified at a 450-hour Pilates teacher training. I just did it because I love Pilates. Pilates is my boyfriend. I had just decided to put a hold on my dating life, so Pilates is my boyfriend, for now.

I have some training under my belt, and having my body is such a great thing. My music clients really like it too because they can see how happy and healthy and positive I am. I think all of my clients are really attracted to my vibe and the vibe that I put out to the world, because it's reflective of them—and on them. I have such a positive aura and mental state at this point, and they really perceive that.

It's been really great to tap into that side of myself and to bring that into what I do as a career, and to have it amplify what I am and what I'm doing in the world. That was my original intention—to make the world a better place with music and to help the artists that make that music.

Helping artists is so fulfilling. I'm really lucky that I haven't had that moment that a lot of my friends did where they just had to get out of the music industry. I'm very entrepreneurial and pragmatic and nimble, and I've been able to pivot; away from the physical vinyl and CDs to all digital; from indie to major, back to indie; always being able to evolve as the business evolves.

It's certainly been a journey, and it's been about starting over. You never think you will have to start over. I've always done what I love, and by always following my passion, I've been really fulfilled—except for that brief eight years when I had a boss. Even then, I learned so much from that experience, and I wouldn't be managing the huge acts that I am today without having had that experience and learning how not to do it.

What's the best or most memorable advice you've received?

Don't get married. Don't marry that guy. Actually, the best advice was when Stu Sobol said, "Just come out here, come out to LA and don't worry about having a job. Just do it, and we'll find something for you." I guess the best advice I ever had was that, and then I did it. I took that chance at the age of 35 with a baby and no job, and I moved across the country, where I had no family, nobody, except for some music industry friends.

What message would you give to the readers of this book about living their best life, whatever that means?

I'd say you have to open up. If you're unhappy in your current situation, there's nothing worse than staying in an unhappy situation. Change is great.

Change is motion. The world exists in a state of flow. I love the theory of flow, being open to things that come into your life for maybe no reason—or you just don't know the reason, and to embrace that because that's what's going to keep things interesting, fluid and juicy—artsy and not stagnant. If you just let change happen, then you don't have to want the change. It becomes part of your life, an ongoing thing, and it's not scary at all. We have to be able to be pragmatic and nimble and open to it, and never be afraid of it, because it's only a good thing.

Great food for thought. How about the best book you've ever read or one that's been memorable?

The Power of Positive Thinking by Norman Vincent Peale. I love that book. I also love *Gone With the Wind* by Margaret Mitchell and anything by Jane Austen.

What life experiences are the ones you feel have shaped really you?

I've got three. Number one: moving around a lot! I had to develop tough skin as a kid. Change happened frequently, and I had to adapt. It kept me on my toes.

Number two: having a child. This taught me patience and generosity. This bond is what a real relationship looks like.

Number three: Most recently, I broke my leg! It humbled me. Just when I think I'm at the top of my game—nope! Life happens—unexpectedly. I've had to gracefully rise again. This accident made me slow down. I was out for about five months. I had to learn to walk again. During this quiet time, I did Reiki healing, meditation, and I've built even stronger trust with my partners to help keep my clients happy and business flowing. Lastly, I talked about positivity already, but I really kept a positive mindset throughout this whole event, and I believe that helped with the care I got in the hospital, and I saw the impact that had on those around me. ■

DEBBIE MINK

Tell me a little bit about you as a kid. What was it like growing up?

I grew up pretty comfortable in a homogeneous suburb in South Jersey right outside of Philadelphia. It was myself, my mom, my dad, my brother—and a dog. I always knew there was something greater, out there beyond the suburb. My parents owned a restaurant in Philadelphia, and that exposed me to a more diverse life experience. I couldn't wait to grow up and bust out of the burbs.

Favorite hobbies? What did you want to be when you grew up?

I danced my whole life. In middle and high school, I danced in the local dance company, and I still take dance classes to this day. I never knew what I wanted to be when I grew up. I just knew I wanted to grow up; to be more independent, to make my own decisions, to have more fun. I used to imagine that I would get discovered just crossing the street. A car would pull over, and someone would hop out and say, "Hey, hey you, you are exactly what we are looking for," and then I would become famous. I also knew that when I graduated college I was going to waitress. I would tell people, "I am going to waitress my way around the world."

Can you share a little bit about your career path? What did that look like?

My career path has been less of a path and more of a career fall! I waitressed for years as I pursued other creative endeavors: I went to art school, I was a spoken word performance artist, an installation artist, a choreographer for a synchronized dance troupe, a ceramicist.

Then, I got repetitive stress injury from waitressing and couldn't even pull my pants up after I went to the bathroom. Once I rehabbed my arms, neck and back, I started working on the sales floor at Betsey Johnson. Pretty soon, I was managing the store. At the same time, I was also starting my own business, manufacturing and selling tampon, condom, and lipstick cases and wallets. They were based on a design I created that incorporated a female mink/human character

named Miz Mink. Miz Mink was all about the power of being female and may have launched a bit before her time. Plus, I knew nothing about wholesale manufacturing or selling to stores, and I couldn't get the business off the ground. So I moved into corporate retail; planning then buying.

Then, I stayed home for a few years with my kids. I found myself getting the itch to get back to work and then got super lucky—I got hired at a tech company as they were starting to build out retail teams. I was a site merchandising manager and third-party seller platform manager for about five years.

I understand you're on a new career/vocation track. What's happening now?

I am now a senior director of marketing. I've found a super creative, fun and demanding job. It taps into a lot of my creative abilities that I hadn't been able to use in the work world until now. For instance, I got to be part of the team that conceptualized, built, painted and installed these awesome walls we used as Instagram backdrops. It brought me way back to when I was in art school. I loved it—plus they were a huge success. I also get to lead a weekly webinar for hundreds of women. That taps into my love of performing and inspiring others.

As far as my personal endeavors, I have launched a podcast called Talking Smack 415, and I am working on a four-year-long project about my response to the election.

What's one life experience that has shaped your character?

This comes to mind: My parents have always been super encouraging of all my creative ideas and passions. Therefore, I have been able to pursue many different paths.

Best advice you've received?

Remember to stay in it and get messy and play—it's part of the process.

Best book you've read?

Sadly, I don't get to read as much as I'd like to, so I am trying to make it more of a priority. I just finished

Elizabeth Gilbert's *City of Girls*—I loved it. I would like to read *Born a Crime* by Trevor Noah, *The Creative Habit* by Twyla Tharp, and *Catching Fire* by Suzanne Collins.

A lesson you've had to learn over and over?

That just because I have an idea doesn't mean I need to act on it and see it through to the end. It can just be an idea, and I can let it go.

What keeps you up at night?

I fall asleep super easily because I get up at the crack of dawn. If I get woken up by my husband, kids, bladder or dog in the middle of the night, I spin out on everything. Most recently I have been worried about my daughter's adjustment to middle school; my son's after school activities; planning their birthday parties; not having my piece ready for the event I am performing at this weekend; asking the landlord to fix our heat and not increasing our rent; not being able to focus enough on the creation of my podcast; what to cook the family for dinner... I'm all over the place. Definitely, first world problems!

What message would you like to share with our readers who might be wondering if they should take a risk into something new?

Do it. It is the same advice I need to tell myself over and over again. Go for it. ∎

@ringletleader   @talkingsmack415 / www.talkingsmack415.com

DENISE AMBROSI

Do you mind telling me a little bit about how you were as a kid, what was it like for you growing up? Did you know what you wanted to be when you grew up?

That's a funny story. So, my mom was an executive secretary, and I used to go with her to work on really special days. All the ladies in her office would swoon over me and want to take me to their cubicles. They would sit me at a typewriter and give me paper, and I would happily click-clack the day away! I never wanted to be a doctor or a veterinarian. I was determined to be a secretary! Luckily, I picked up on a lot of my mom's other skills and soaked up all of her creative genes too!

I associate you with being an artist. How did that play into your childhood, if at all?

My mom was and still is super crafty. She was always sewing and crocheting. I remember taking a crocheting class when I was in kindergarten and then going to the Renaissance fair as a kid in costumes handmade by my mom. My second career option was going to be something with alterations or fashion design.

Were those your hobbies, making stuff with your mom?

My mom had such an influence over the person that I've become. I feel that I'm doing the same thing with my daughter Amelia. I just teach her all of the things that I like to do, and she just soaks it all up! I wish I still had my Holly Hobbie sewing machine to give to her!

Can you share a little bit about your career path and beginnings as a working adult?

Before I went to college, I was in sewing classes throughout high school, and I started getting into making my own jewelry. I worked for a coffee shop, and they encouraged me to display my jewelry to sell in their shop. I don't remember anything selling, but that was my first real memory of being supported in my craft. I went to college, even though it wasn't my first choice. My parents kind of pushed me toward it, but all I wanted to do was art. I went in with a business major, and maybe a semester in, I switched my major

to art. My parents didn't support this decision, so I was forced to switch back to a more "acceptable" profession.

After college, I had several jobs that paid the rent, but all I wanted to do was create. I was determined to have a creative profession, so I quit my job and started selling my art and jewelry at art shows and farmers markets. It was exhausting work; setting up and breaking down my booth, rain or shine, hot or freezing cold. Then, the bruised ego if you didn't sell enough a particular day. It's hard to put yourself out there! I did that for about a year until my back was killing me, and I ran out of money.

I've been trying to push my jewelry ever since then. I think I just realized that I don't care about the marketing, the selling…the business piece. I just have this desire to create. I don't care about selling it. Selling it is a means to pay for the hobby—at least I can say that now. I think if I were in a different situation, maybe I would feel differently about it, but I know that now I just need to create; that's the bottom line. I don't have to be famous. I don't have to be known for my jewelry; I just need to make it.

What's on the horizon for you now?

My next idea is building this community of artists and makers by opening my makers' club. This is just going to be me surrounding myself with other creative people, which will feed my desire to create more, all the time. I don't know if it'll be a viable business, but the bottom line is that if it can pay for itself, then I'll be able to do some really cool things that I'm excited about—and I won't have to worry about sales.

What led you to pivot into this idea of community?

I would say—a thousand percent—reading Elizabeth Gilbert's *Big Magic*. It led me to the idea of living a life of creativity. After reading it, I started writing out what my dream life would look like. I wrote that I wanted to have a retail shop with a studio space. The reality of it is, I'm just trying to figure out a way to pay for my hobby, to pay for my art. I don't know how it's going to work; how will I afford the rent for a space? Who will come? From there, it has kind of morphed into,

do not pursue the past.
do not lose yourself
in the future - the
past is no longer.
the future has not
yet come. we must
be diligent today.
to wait until
tomorrow is too late.

-BHADDEKARATTA
SUTTA

well, I just want to have a workshop space, that's what I want.

It's so funny because this could easily be a business, and it's doing exactly what I want to do, yet it feels like what I did 15 years ago, when I worked at The Coffee Bean, having craft parties. That's basically what this is; it would be a dream to be able to do something like that full time.

It feels like it's the right time, I'm seeing a lot of similar things right now as I did then. I'm still doing my research, and I'm not going to worry about other people that have done it before me. I wrote down a quote from *Big Magic* that says, "Everything has been done before, but it hasn't been done by you." I just keep reminding myself of this.

Love it, love it. Looking forward to seeing what unfolds! Now I kind of have more life questions. What's some memorable advice you've received?

The best advice that I've received is to create something every single day that you breathe. Whatever it is that you want to do, do it every day whether you feel like it or not, and it will feed you—it will breathe life into you.

I did a 365-day ring-making challenge, which is another thing that made me realize that I have to exercise and to build up this creative muscle.

What's the best book you've read?

The best book that I have read by far is *Big Magic*.

What's the lesson that you have learned over and over again?

Probably to not take things personally. I'm super attached emotionally to anything I create. I just have such a strong reaction if someone doesn't like it or doesn't love it. Another quote from the book was "If someone doesn't like what you're doing, it's none of your business." It's actually none of your business what other people think of your work. It's your job to make it and then to let it go; then make something else and let that go.

What message would you like to give our readers who are on the fence about trying something new?

Believe in yourself and just continue to do what you love. Whatever idea you think you're going to do, think about it for a year, and if you still like it in a year, then go for it. Make sure that it's something that feeds you. Do your homework; do your artwork daily and keep doing it even if it's not going to make the money, even if it's not impressing anybody, but you just keep practicing. ■

@thesehandscollective   /thesehandsmakerscollective/   email: denise@thesehandscollective.com

ELLEN STERN

Can you tell me a little bit about you as a child? What was it like growing up?

I grew up in St. Louis, Missouri. Initially, I had an idealistic and carefree childhood, but I learned at an early age that life can change in the blink of an eye. My dad tragically died shortly before my 12th birthday, when he fell down an elevator shaft. That sort of shock to the system is a childhood trauma I've had to deal with. It changed the course of my whole life. When you're a child, still so full of innocence and wonder and then such a tragic loss happens in such a horrible manner, you kind of have to grow up quickly.

I have a lot of memory loss. I couldn't recall events from the two years around the accident because I was so sad and depressed. Those memories started coming to me in dreams, and with the work of a good therapist as well as my family confirming that my dreams were indeed memories, those lost two years returned. I've learned that memory loss was what people now called PTSD, post-traumatic stress disorder.

Because of the trauma, I was really depressed and eventually started self-medicating. I was so sad, but I saw that everyone around me was happy, and I found out they were smoking pot. I started smoking pot because I just wanted to laugh and be happy.

Did you know when you were little what you wanted to be when you grew up?

I had to write an autobiography in fourth grade. There were four things I wanted to be: a secretary, a nurse, an artist, or a teacher. From the beginning, it was a lot of creativity and helping people. I guess I had a vision board before I knew what a vision board was.

Can you share a little bit about your work and career path?

I knew that I had a creative gift, but I didn't really know what I wanted to do with that. I had my first job as a hostess in a restaurant at 14. I was mature-looking for my age, so I passed for 16.

I stayed in the restaurant business for 17 years, eventually bartending and running a restaurant. I went to a lot of different colleges and took classes that interested me, but I always loved doing art. At some point, I got out of the restaurant business, and my mom was like, "You have to get a career in art, get a degree in art." So, I went to graphic design school.

While I was in school, I worked at a golf course. I was the "beer cart girl." It paid well, and I had fun. When I finished graphic design school, I started working at a magazine. I kept the golf course job part time. I worked as a graphic designer for about five to 10 years. As an artist, it wasn't fulfilling, because I worked at a magazine—there was pressure, deadlines; advertisements that needed to get placed. I stopped doing my own fine art because I was on the computer all day. When I got home, being creative was the last thing I wanted to do, and my own art kind of went by the wayside.

What happened next?

I had another life-defining moment. I got hit in the head with a golf ball! My head had to get stapled back together. I thought I was OK, but I noticed years later that I was just in the biggest brain fog when I was doing graphic design. I was in a huge depression, crying every day for no reason. And so, I told my boss, and my boss took me to the doctor, who said, "Oh, it sounds psychological, you need to go to the shrink." And the shrink said, "We need to medicate you." I wasn't a believer in having to take pharmaceuticals every day, but I didn't want to be depressed either. I asked her what else I could do, and she said I could do biofeedback or neurofeedback. She made it sound really scary like I was going to be stuck with all these wires—it's nothing like that.

I took the recommended medication for one year, even though I know it's not good for your liver and kidneys. It did help with the depression, but it actually just made me not feel anything. I wasn't crying, but I really wasn't feeling anything.

It's funny how the universe provides guidance when you're supposed to do something. I had put an ad on Craigslist looking for a roommate. This woman answered my ad—she was coming down to Pasadena to study biofeedback and neurofeedback.

While we didn't become roommates, this healing angel of a woman hooked me up to the neurofeedback machine. She asked me, "Oh, have you had any brain injuries, head traumas?" I'm like, "Yeah, yeah."

She rewired my brain. After three sessions I started to get focus and clarity back. It was amazing! I knew I wanted to do this to help other people. This path to healing by noninvasively retraining people's brains resonated with me.

And so, I learned how to do biofeedback. I was so happy being able to help other people. I trained with her and then, after a year, I got my own equipment and opened my own practice. I continued training with different mentors and got certified through the school, the manufacturer, and the people who make the equipment. Since I got my own equipment in 2005, I've worked on thousands of people.

The biggest blessing is that for the last several years, I've had the time and creative inspiration for my artwork. My art can now be seen in shows put on by the Hollywood galleries that represent me.

What life experiences have really shaped your character?

I had a very active, fun life, but trauma definitely shaped my childhood. When you lose a parent and experience trauma in such formative years, it makes a difference in who you are and how you show up in the world. Getting married and divorced has certainly shaped me also.

After my divorce, just like Eat Pray Love, I went to India several times, where I learned meditation and mantras and worked on my spiritual path. Obtaining that path to being centered shaped this version of me.

Is there any advice that you've received from a teacher or mentor that still sticks with you?

Yes, the artist Rassouli was a huge influence. In my art, I was more of a landscape, watercolor painter, painting nature scenes. When I started painting with Rassouli, he said, "You have to paint from your heart. Paint from within." So, that advice expanded my art style.

I've been blessed to manifest master teachers my whole life. The Rev. Michael Beckwith from Agape International Spirit Center changed my life. He came into my life when I was making the shift with biofeedback from graphic design. His advice was "Dive deep." He is still a huge mentor to me.

It really makes a difference when you're following your passion. If you take a leap of faith and step into that, then everything manifests easier.

What book has made an impact on you?

Conversations With God by Neale Donald Walsch; books one, two and three of his series had a huge impact on me. His teaching of thoughts, words, actions will stay with me forever. Others that come to mind are *The Celestine Prophecy* by James Redfield and *The Power of the Subconscious Mind* by Joseph Murphy.

Is there a lesson you've had to learn over and over again?

Discernment. Yeah, my grandmother, God bless her, saw the world through rose-colored glasses. I definitely have that trait and characteristics. Sometimes I see the good in everybody, and sometimes I can be fooled. I've had to learn to listen to my intuition because not everybody necessarily has the best intentions.

I'm so energetically sensitive that when I don't listen to my inner guidance, I always end up asking myself, "Ah, why didn't I listen?"

What message would you like to leave with our readers who are on the fence about trying something new or going for what they're really passionate about?

I'd say, follow your heart and your inner guidance and do what brings you joy and passion. You will be supported. For those who are looking to make a career change, do the internship, shadow somebody in a field that interests you. I'll pass along Rev. Michael's words: "Dive deep." ∎

@ellensternbiofeedback   www.biofeedbackmatters.com

THOUGHT IS THE FIRST LEVEL OF CREATION. NEXT COMES THE WORD. EVERYTHING YOU SAY IS A THOUGHT EXPRESSED. IT IS CREATIVE & SENDS FORTH ENERGY INTO THE UNIVERSE. WORDS ARE THE SECOND LEVEL OF CREATION. NEXT COMES ACTION. —NEALE DONALD WALSCH

EMILY HARMAN

Tell me a little bit about you as a kid. What was growing up like for you?

I am the oldest of three children. My brother is 18 months younger than me, and my sister is three years younger. We had a nice childhood. Strict parents. Summer camps—six weeks away—many summers. Our parents took us hiking and emphasized sports and reading and healthy eating.

Favorite hobbies?

I played basketball and soccer and ran track. I was a star basketball player in high school.

Did you know what you wanted to be when you grew up?

No. My parents don't remember me mentioning anything, and my sister doesn't either. I have a feeling I did not think about stuff like that, and I did not have big dreams.

Can you share a little bit about your career path? What did that look like?

I graduated from the Naval Academy in 1985. I was a Supply Corps officer in the Navy; on active duty for seven years and in the reserves for 13. I was stationed on a ship from 1986 to 1988. I worked as a civilian for the Navy beginning in 1992 and retired in May 2019. I'm currently a senior executive serving as Director of Small Business Programs for the Navy and Marine Corps.

I heard you might be making a shift in career/life? Can you share what sparked that change?

I realized that I have been working for the Navy since I started college in 1981, and I wanted to do something different. I'm allowing myself to dream and to act on those dreams. My children are 22 and 25. I was a single parent for many years and did what I had to do. Now I intend to do what I want to do. I'm not sure that I really know who I am. I have overcome so many obstacles and challenges in my life, and I want to start a podcast to help others do the same.

What's a life experience that has shaped your character?

Graduating from the Naval Academy in the sixth class of women to graduate.

Best or memorable advice you've received?

Always take advantage of your opportunities. My father told me that.

Best book you've read (or one that just really made an impact on you)?

All of Eckhart Tolle's books. Be in the moment.

What is a lesson you've had to learn over and over?

To make time to exercise and to take time for myself without feeling guilty.

What message would you like to impart to our readers who are in their 40s and on the fence about trying something new or going for something they are passionate about?

If you are passionate about it, it won't feel like a job. Start off as a side hustle, if necessary. Don't wait for everything to be perfect. Action brings clarity. ∎

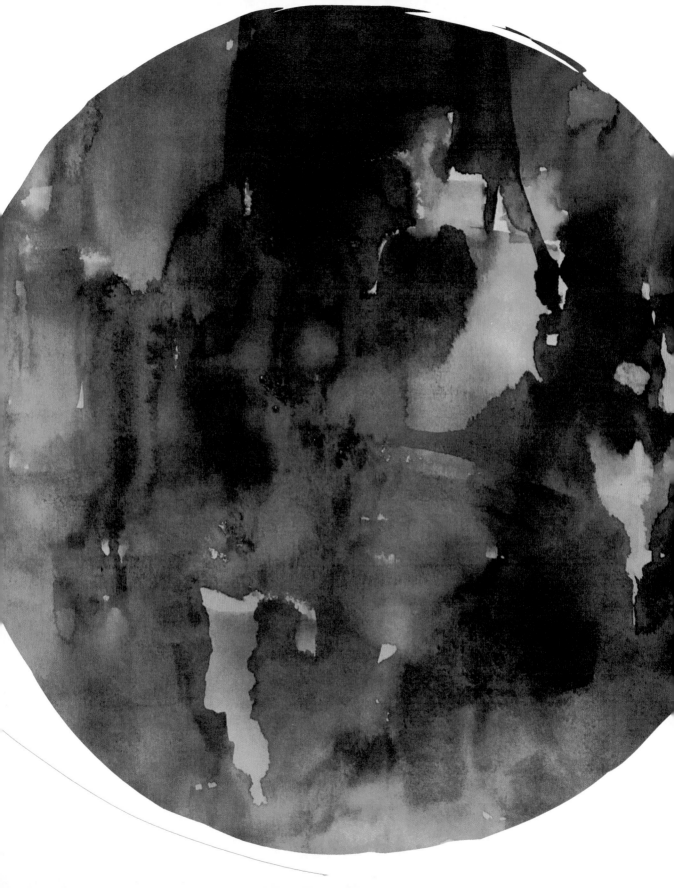

JULIETA LIMA

Tell me a little bit about you as a kid. What was it like for you growing up? Favorite hobbies? Did you know what you wanted to be when you grew up?

I actually had a very nice childhood, loving parents and siblings. I'm the youngest, and I was very introverted—still am—and my sister was the opposite. I do remember being the quiet one and also trying to stay out of the way. I didn't want to be a problem for my parents. I felt that they had their hands full with my siblings, so I spent a lot of time alone, mostly daydreaming. I knew I wanted to be an artist, but being a part of a struggling middle-class family, I felt I had to find something with a clear path to employment.

Can you share a little bit about your career path? What did that look like?

I went to film school thinking that it would be a good compromise. There are many careers within filmmaking, and it seemed that there were places that I could knock at the door and ask for a job. I still took some art classes on the side, but eventually, I stopped. I came to the United States in 2001 from Argentina got took a certificate in entertainment from the UCLA extension…it used to be just be called an entertainment certificate. Now it's is labeled to specific fields: directing, acting, etc. I worked in a few movies as a production assistant and script supervisor, and then I decided to go back to Argentina. I started working as a freelancer. I was an assistant director, and I hated it. So, I then decided to come back to Los Angeles and try it here. I eventually became a script supervisor. Now I work in commercials as a script supervisor. In 2014, I started taking art classes in Hollywood, and that's when things started to shift. I couldn't lie to myself anymore—I realized that drawing, painting and designing are what I love the most, so I kept going and took more classes.

I believe you made a career change at 40. Can you tell me about that pivot?

I decided to open my Etsy shop in 2018, where I sell art prints and do commission work, and I love it. I'm just starting, so I can't say "no" to script supervising jobs just yet, But I'm confident that it will happen in the near future.

It was a long process, but I think that the seed that started the whole thing was when a friend of mine asked me if I could do a drawing of her dog and then another friend did, and so on. That's when I thought, maybe this could be a thing…

What's one life experience that has shaped your character?

I honestly couldn't tell you one life experience that impacted me at that level. Many small things have shaped me. I have to say I was very lucky to have incredibly supportive and loving parents in my life.

What is some memorable advice you've received?

You put yourself in this position; you can remove yourself from it as well.

Best book you've read?

There are so many…one that helped me most recently is *You Are a Badass* by Jen Sincero.

What is a lesson you've had to learn over and over?

I am still learning it—that it is possible to make a livelihood by doing what you love. I always felt that it was something reserved for a very small group of people, like winning the lottery.

What message would you like to impart to our readers who are on the fence about trying something new or going for something they are passionate about?

I can't guarantee that you will succeed in pursuing your passion, but I can guarantee that you will regret it if you don't go for it.

Also: Stop overthinking; it just leads to talking yourself out of taking a risk. ∎

@paintedlives   www.julietalima.com

You Miss 100%
OF THE SHOTS
YOU DONT TAKE.

-WAYNE GRETSKY

the cure for
EVERYTHING
is salt water :
sweat, tears,
or the sea.

- ISAK DINESEN

KATHERINE BELL

Tell me a little bit about you as a kid. What was it like for you growing up? What did you want to be when you grew up? Favorite hobbies?

I grew up as the middle child of three children in Hamilton, Ontario, near Toronto. My parents split, and my mom put herself through school. We were supported by grandparents, too. The lessons I learned quickly were about hard work, family and sacrifice. In our family, we had to triage what was needed. My mom's attention went to my younger brother. My sister and I took a back seat, which made us more independent.

I had no idea what I wanted to be when I grew up. When I got a little older, I wanted to be an international lawyer or a translator. I loved languages, so I learned French and ended up living in France for a little while.

Can you share a little bit about your career path? What did that look like?

I worked in psych research for the Canadian Cancer Society and Smokers' Helpline, as a research assistant in family medicine. I studied social work, and I did a missionary trip which got me interested in family medicine. Eventually, I went to medical school to become a family doctor. It wasn't the career I expected it to be, and I became disillusioned and burned out. I backed away from medicine, changing to part-time work, and began exploring other neglected parts of myself. My intuition said, "This isn't it for you." I want to explore writing. I lost writing over the years and have gotten back into it the last three years. I want to do something that will weave writing with international medicine.

I believe you recently transitioned out of a relationship. Can you share a little bit about that?

In my marriage, I had a hard time; I couldn't talk with him about things the same way as I did with people at work and elsewhere. And my temper came back. I had that as a little kid—anger issues at home. Those two things led me to ask about counseling. Family members who loved me saw a difference when I was with my husband. I didn't see the red flags when we

were dating. Looking back, the signs were there: his previous relationships, his relationships with his family, his drinking.

I had a business partner with whom he was good friends. Their friendship helped me see what was happening with my marriage—the abuse at home. I spoke with a therapist. The therapist suggested I read some books, and I saw my marriage in the books. I realized it wasn't going to get better. I could choose: stay and die or leave. I left three times. I had no trouble standing up for myself in other situations but not with my husband.

During our initial separations, before I realized my partner was abusive, I thought that if I could find the right words to explain how I was feeling and what I needed, we could be OK. But I could never find those words. Everything I did or said seemed to make it worse. The only thing I seemed to be able to do to make it better was to not be there. I felt responsible for the marriage's lack of success. I see now that part of the abuse was gaslighting, making me feel responsible for things not in my control. Still, I stayed in it to try and convince him. I came back in the middle of our custody battle, but unsurprisingly, the issues between us did not resolve. During this period, I learned more about emotional abuse and realized this was what our marriage was about.

What helped me stay away was having no contact with him. We only communicated through email. The cost for me was losing my community, stepchildren and my in-laws. Post-divorce, I still lived in the same area. I had to decide: move or sell my practice. I transitioned out of the business partnership and sold it. I hoped to keep my relationship with my two step-kids, as I had raised them for 10 years. I made a conscious decision to stop the one-sided communication—pursuing them without them communicating back to me. But I keep an open door—I want to be there for them but have had to accept that the paths they are on, whether by choice or because of the situation, may not make it possible. I spent six months preparing to move to Vancouver Island, and I did it.

How are you doing since the move?

I was really surprised by how my loneliness factored into starting a brand-new life. I think that I expected it to some degree, but I also started to feel more compelled to reach out to new friends and start forming new relationships. I felt that was a good sign of healing because I had put a lot of really strong walls and barriers around myself protecting myself previously, and I had to take those down.

It's been nice to relax a little bit this past year, partly due to being in a brand-new environment across the country from my ex and his family, and partly due to the fact that pressures of my day-to-day life aren't affecting them or getting back to them or having repercussions. I think it's also a sign of readiness about being able to start to form those relationships again and to be able to feel those needs again.

I always knew I would probably want to date again, to be married again at some point. I want to share my life with someone else again. It's been just over four years since my separation. We all have our timelines in our head, and we think we should be over things faster than the healing process allows.

The other thing that I'm still struggling with, which I expected to be able to solve so much more easily than I have, has been my physical body and my weight. I've been telling myself a story about how, when my stressful marriage is over, this problem will resolve itself. The hard reality is that it hasn't, because the habits that I formed to cope during those times of stress are still with me.

For me, there's often this element of hypocrisy—because I work in medicine for a living—I'm often giving good advice about diet and exercise and how weight impacts health. So, I find it really hard to do that when I'm unhappy with my body. I feel very hypocritical. It's been an interesting little dive into looking at how I view myself through a shameful lens.

I would love for this not to be an issue, but probably for the majority of women it is—at some point in their life they are not able to gain weight or lose weight as they would like. I'm frustrated that's still something I'm wrestling with, but I think it's an important part

of healing. So, that's one of the things I'm trying to address right now—how to live in a healthy way and ultimately have the body that I feel comfortable in and that I'm proud of. This body is not going to last for a lifetime if I don't begin to treat it better than it is, and the decisions I make today will really determine how good my life is when I'm 60, 70, 80.

Lastly, since my separation, I've had creative bursts. I've had room and space timewise but also emotionally and spiritwise to be so much more creative in my work life, in my writing and in visual arts. I started experimenting with painting and making a quilt and doing all sorts of really interesting things that I haven't really tried before.

And that was one of the really lovely surprises about ending a difficult relationship, to have the energy to do these things and also just the intellectual and emotional space to consider things in a way that I haven't for a long time.

Writing has always been a part of my life. I've always journaled, and I've always done writing projects. But visual art was something that I wouldn't have tried really; it's like one of those things you do in middle school and then you get to ninth grade.

I'd always wanted to read the Julia Cameron book, *The Artist's Way*. I had bought it, but I wanted to start it with a group, and I started to envision what it would be like to create a group at my local library and my local church and meet some people around me. It didn't work that way, but I connected with someone through a writing group on Facebook, and she and I worked together and have become…we're not writing partners in the sense that we write together, but we're definitely friends, and we're creative accountability partners.

We touch base on what we're doing in our writing, what we're doing creatively, how things are rippling in our life or where we're stuck. And that's been really cool to have connections that that are based on these whole new realms of my life, like creativity and figuring out where I want to be artistic and how am I artistic and creating that little tide together to support me back.

Advice for our readers, who may be in a similar situation?

Admit what you are in the middle of. With relationships, no one thing on its own looks abusive. Emotional abuse is hard to define. If you have a doubt, there's probably something there. You deserve the time and effort to look at what is going on. Explore what makes you happy. It isn't about how smart or successful you are. It doesn't matter how good of a person you are. It's not your failure. Can he be different, or will he be different? "Can't" or "won't" become irrelevant. Express your feelings.

Best or most memorable advice you've received?

One: There is always a choice. I was making an active choice every day. You're one decision away from a different life… We have choices. During times of frustration, you have a choice.

Two: Can't or won't—it doesn't matter. You need to show up.

Three: Be in a place where you are biased for risk. What will you lose? Don't ask yourself "why?" but "why not?" If there isn't a good reason not to do it, then try it. Take the risk.

Four (advice from my mom): Don't worry if there are jobs in a particular field. Do what you love, and your passion will translate. There will always be room for good people, even if the field seems full. Don't worry about enough, worry about what we really love to do. There will be room. Bring your gifts.

Five: Career pathway: How do you pick? Don't ask, is this the right path? Is there any reason not to take this path?

Best books you've read?

The Dance of Anger by Harriette Lerner and *Codependent No More* by Melody Beattie.

What is the lesson you've had to learn over and over?

Be comfortable not being in control. I wanted to be the leader and get things done. There's a dark side to that: I took responsibility for things that weren't mine.

Work lesson: Not my circus, not my monkeys. I can step back. I don't need to fix it. Be comfortable not being in control.

And also: Learn to be OK with people suffering the consequences of their own actions and decisions. ∎

@bellkatherinef   email: bellkatherinef@gmail.com

KERRYN VAUGHAN

Is there anything you want to share from your life while you were growing up?

I've got a very boring childhood. I was raised in a great family with four younger sisters. As the oldest, we're the trailblazers—or the ones that get in all the trouble. I lived in a country town with around 7,000 people. I had friends, but I often chose to be on my own as I preferred playing with my pets more than I did other kids. I would take my cat on the skateboard and take my rabbit on the bike, tucked up into my sweater.

I also wanted to play guitar. My neighbor played guitar, and she yodeled. I used to say, "Oh, I want to do that!" After a fair bit of whining, Mum finally said, "When you're 7, you can have a guitar." I turned 7 and, true to her word, she got me a guitar. It was one that nearly cut my fingers every time I played the damn thing. I spent most of my childhood playing guitar and imagining I was going to be a rock star.

I played sports as well, but in those days everyone did. I was always a real tomboy, so while the girls were playing with their Barbie dolls and crap, I was playing with my Matchbox and Hot Wheels cars. I had all these collections—a stamp collection, a coin collection and a beach shell collection. As I got older, I even had a beer can collection.

I loved inventing things. I pulled things apart to see how they worked. I spent lots of time in the shed. Mum would say, "Where have you been?" and my answer would never impress her. Particularly once when my response was, "Building a cubby." A cubby is like a playhouse. The look on Mum's face was priceless, and the conversation went like this:

Mum: "Where did you build a cubby?"
Kerryn: "Around the side of the house."
Mum: "What did you use?"
Kerryn: "A shovel."
Mum: "What do you mean a shovel?"
Kerryn: "I—I dug a hole. It's an underground cubby."

She came outside to check out the 6-foot by 6-foot hole I was so proud of. Mum was not as impressed and went on to protest, "You can't be in there, it'll collapse, you'll die, you'll suffocate."

I used to get the paint out of the shed and paint the house, and Mum would come out yelling, "Oh, stop painting the house! It's a different color!" I was naughty, but I didn't think I was being naughty. Maybe it was more curiosity than naughtiness. Remember what I said about the oldest child? I was always the one getting in trouble!

I also really loved school. I was really bright, and in second grade, I had a teacher whose husband played football with my dad. The couple used to come to my house every Saturday night after the game. She'd sit on my bed and read me a book, and I felt like the most special student in the class. But then she moved away, and Dad said that she'd had a car accident on the way to where she was moving to, and she lost her kidney. As a 7-year-old, I didn't understand this and was so upset because they couldn't find her kidney. They weren't looking hard enough: Where is it? Why didn't they look for it?

Her replacement was a crabby teacher and then I hated school. I was just lucky to be bright enough to get through, but my favorite teacher was gone. After that, education didn't mean that much to me. I learned all the important things from home and from experience.

How about transitioning into work, how was that?

I didn't go back to complete my last year of secondary school. I wanted to be a teacher, but when I was 15, I wanted an electric guitar. Mum said, "No, I've already bought you a guitar." I said, "But I can't use it Mum. I've had it for eight years." She said, "Well, you have to get a job." So over the summer holidays, I got a job at a supermarket and was earning $7 a week. I thought, "Wow, this is awesome. I'm going to be a millionaire in no time. I'm going to keep doing this work thing." I didn't care that it was a supermarket—I cared that I was making money. Every week I would go to the music shop and pay $7 off my layaway until I finally had that guitar and amp. That $7 was my whole week's wage and that was the

Those who mind don't matter & those who matter don't mind.

— DR. SEUSS

best lesson I ever learned in my life. I was patient, determined and learned the value of money. When that $7-a-week part-time job eventually turned into a $74-dollars-a-week full-time job, I saw no point in returning to school.

After that, I did a lot of odd jobs. If I ever had enough of the boss, I would just go and get another job. I've always had that attitude—"I'm sick of this job; I'm sick of that boss; I'm sick of that person. I'm just going to go and do something else." I had so many jobs, but boy, do I have a great bucket of skills!

But I always had it in my mind that I was going to be a rock star. I kept my eye firmly on Suzy Quatro as my hero—I was going to be just like her. It didn't matter what job I was doing, because they were just paying the bills while I was getting ready to be a rock star. I worked for the post office; I made umbrellas; I washed cars. Whatever I could as a means to an end.

Then, in my 30s, my younger sister was diagnosed with cancer. That put a whole different spin on things. I felt I needed to settle down a bit to help her, as she had three little kids. Her husband wasn't any help, and in fact, was like a fourth child, as he had been in a serious car accident and had a brain injury. I was working about an hour away from my hometown so I decided to move back. She fought bravely for around five years but finally lost her battle.

I'd always wanted to work with people with disabilities, but I never had a chance because it meant finding a year to do a disability course full time. That meant no income. But after my sister died, I was pissed off at the world and thought, "I don't care about work. I'm just going to go and do this course because that's what I want to do."

A few months into the course, I got a job in the disability field, and the following year, I became a disability teacher. I was teaching certification to students who would end up working with people with disabilities, and I became specialized in autism and behavior.

My sister died when I was 39, so I dilly-dallied around for another 11 years, but by the time I got to 50, I looked back at the many amazing things I had done in my life. But what struck me was that I didn't really have a record of any of them. No legacy. That made me start questioning a lot of things. While I was teaching autism and behavior training, I'd go into schools, training staff to work with these kids. Some teachers would say to me, "You have to fix these kids." That really got under my skin, because I thought, "They're not broken, there's nothing wrong with these kids." I then sort of combined my need to have a legacy with my need to show that these kids weren't broken.

The outcome was my first book, *Magnificent Kids!* I interviewed 23 kids from around the world who had set up world-changing projects before the age of 18. I wanted the world to acknowledge kids' strengths and to start focusing on teaching kids how to think instead of what to think. The world's in an interesting state, and if we don't give support for the next generation to care deeply, we're screwed.

That's amazing. Where did this book take you next?

When I did my book launch, I had a picture taken with a friend. We were both holding the book. She had a friend in Africa who saw the photo, and he wanted to know where he could get the book. He's a teacher in Guinea, so I sent him a copy. He was so inspired that he started a "magnificent class" at his school. He then asked if I would Skype with his students and, of course, I agreed. I then got a little excited and suggested I get a couple of the kids from the book to Skype with his class as well. But then I went even further, and those who know me, know that I tend to jump in before I have logistics all worked out. I suggested his class in Africa Skype with a class in Australia. Great! We both loved this idea!

He then told me he didn't have a laptop, so I put a call out on Facebook and ended up with 30. I thought, "Well, I'd better start up an organization." So, I started One Planet Classrooms and within two weeks of starting it, I had 45 schools enrolled.

My first thought was, "Shit! This is going to be big!"

Then I decided to research getting the laptops to Uganda, but disappointment soon kicked in. It was going to cost $600 to fly each one in because of the lithium batteries—a nightmare. So, this was not going to be an easy venture nor would it be affordable. We did eventually find a way to get 28 laptops into Kenya, then 20 over to Uganda.

Ultimately, it was an absolute failure for three reasons: First, it was near impossible to supply them with laptops because of the logistics. Second, when the kids are in school in Africa, the kids are not in school in Australia, they're in bed. And finally, I sent laptops to a country where 95% of the people don't have power!

Epic failure! So, I sought to find a lesson in all that. I could either say, "Oh, well, I screwed up," and run away with my tail between my legs, or say, "Well, what did I learn?"

What I learned was that many kids were dying from drinking dirty, stagnant water. They're getting water in these great big jerry cans from stagnant ponds full of parasites. The cattle are using it for a toilet, men are distilling alcohol on the other side of the water, and they're peeing in it. Kids are dying! My only thought was, "Well, now that I have access to all these teachers and all these great people in Africa, I'm just going to ask them what they need, and I'm just going to get it done."

Also, the girls are the ones who have to walk miles and miles to fetch water. It's always a girl's job, but on the way, they're often sexually assaulted. They're paid for sex, or they exchange sex for sanitary items, and even very young girls are raped and assaulted.

It is a great lesson to realize that helping people really is so simple. We tend to think everything's complicated. But if I look back at what has been achieved, it's massive. Since 2015, we have completed over 40 major projects: water tanks into schools; water wells into villages and communities; mattresses, mosquito nets, blankets. We even bought several blocks of land to help rebuild a school and set up women's empowerment projects. We've also put solar systems in schools so that the kids can stay at school and study for three weeks when it's exam time and actually pass. Otherwise, if the girls don't make it to secondary school, they're married off as young as 11-12 years old—not good at all.

We've helped well over 3,000 girls stay in school by supplying sanitary items and undies, and we also have a student sponsorship program with 180 enrolled.

Then in 2018, I was at an International Women's Day event. I was coaching a table, and there were all these cards on the table like, "I promise to stand up for women." "I promise to speak out." "I promise to…" But then I found one that really resonated with me and provided a serious challenge: "I will launch a purposeful, female-focused initiative." I then got up on stage in front of 300 women and said, "I'm going to…" Yet again, I jumped in without thinking. I left the stage and thought, "Oh, shit. Now, I've got to do it because I'm accountable to 300 women." That was when I launched Girls with Hammers with my partner.

That's fantastic. You just don't stop!
Very admirable.

We're focusing on conferences and workshops. Our first conference was in October 2018. With six speakers, they inspired women and gave them tools and strategies for empowerment.

In 2019, I finished my second book, *Get Off the Bench*, which is about kick-starting your idea or project. It helps you to get an idea out of your head and into action. I facilitate public and corporate workshops under this banner and topic, and that's going extremely well.

What's next?

I also wanted to do a podcast. I told my partner, Nicky, "I'm starting a podcast." She said, "What do you mean you're starting a podcast? You can't just start a podcast." I said, "Watch me!" So, I started one with Campbell Remess from Project 365. We've done a few episodes and it's called *Kerryn with Bumble*. Admittedly, we're still trying to get it right. We're still learning our skills and getting our equipment right, and somehow overcoming our challenge of living in different states. The other challenge is that we are both so busy, we struggle to find available time slots where both of us and a guest can all be available at once. But we were not going to wait for perfect. Who knows if we can push our way through the challenges, but life's about backing yourself up and starting! I have an "I can" attitude, and I'm not going to let anyone stop me.

I will be launching my podcast in 2020, and I am very much looking forward to that. That will likely focus on people doing great things and how they "got off the bench." But I have to find some spare time to prepare a bit to ensure its longevity.

What advice would you give women who might be wondering what kind of difference they can make in the world?

I think anybody at any age can make a difference. Believing it's possible because anything is possible. Saying "I can." Once you decide to do something, the universe makes it happen anyway, but you have to say it out loud. That's a great way to hear it and to help overcome things like imposter syndrome. When you hear yourself saying it, it doesn't feel anywhere near as big, scary or impossible. Take the first step, then the next. Just back yourself!

The other thing is to live life like you're already doing that thing. Design the life you imagine; the life you want and then work out the steps. Every time you take a step into that life, you're being true to you.

What life experience shaped your character?

Losing my sister has made me determined to leave a legacy.

Best book you've read or listened to lately?

I hardly read books. I love starting them and then I find another one! I rarely finish one.

Does anything keep you up at night?

Thinking of ideas, planning ways to make the world a better place, trying to figure out how mechanical things work, trying to think of ways we can get the next generation to understand how important it is to make a difference.

How about a lesson that you've had to learn over and over?

Trust your gut. Do what your gut tells you to do, because whenever we go, "Oh, I'd like to or I should, but what if I...," then the head starts. As soon as my head starts, I tell it, "No, I don't want to talk about it now, I'm done." Then I'll come back to it. It's kind of like a silly game, but it works. I pretend to sneak off without my head and let it catch up later. We should use our hearts to make decisions and our heads to plan out the steps. ∎

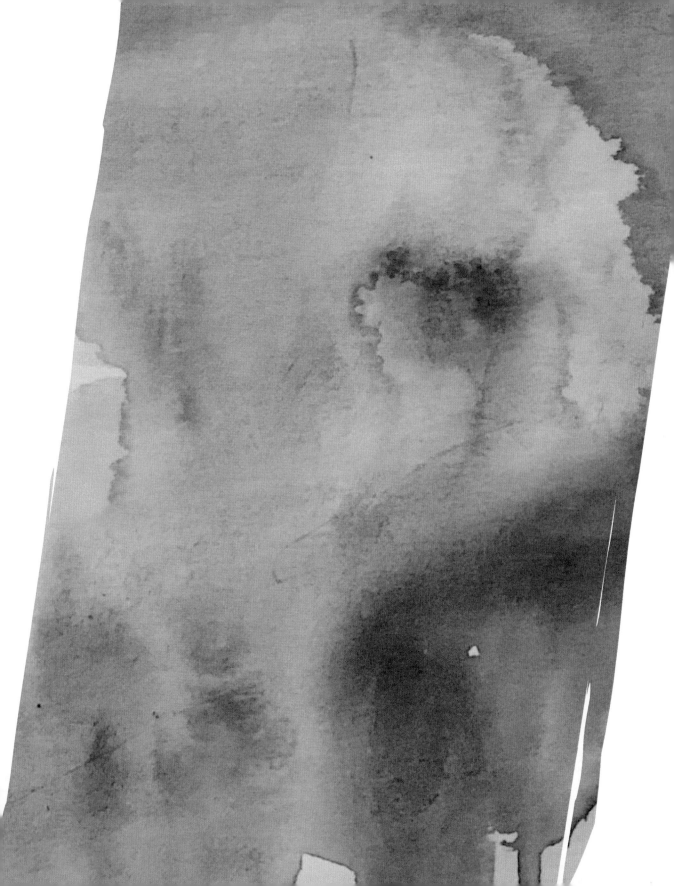

do the best
you can until
you know better.
then when you
know better,
do better.

— MAYA
ANGELOU

LAURIE KNAUP

Tell me a little bit about your early life. What was it like growing up? Did you know what you wanted to be when you grew up?

I was born in Hayward, California, outside Oakland, but then we moved to Anaheim. My dad worked, and I had a stay-at-home mom. I had a good upbringing, what I'd call a normal life. Then my parents divorced unexpectedly when I was 17.

When I was little, I thought I'd be a teacher. I got accepted to Cal State Long Beach, and after two semesters, I decided college wasn't for me, so I started working. I've had seven jobs in my entire life. I tend to find places that feel like family. I met some of my best friends at those jobs.

Do you have any favorite hobbies?

I love to read and to listen to music. Anything from Billie Holiday to Green Day.

Where are you now?

I currently live in Washington state.

What led up to that move?

I was searching for another opportunity within the amazing company I work for. There came a point where I wanted more growth, and California was getting too expensive! I had to be open to the possibility of moving out of state. I've never lived outside of California, and that was a huge moment for me. My husband and I decided to and pick up and move. My whole life was in California. That's where I had roots. Leaving family and friends was a huge ordeal.

How was that process for you—deciding where to move?

The opportunity presented itself three times. It was a matter of deciding where in the United States to go. The first opportunity was in Georgia. We ended up not pursuing that because the lifestyle wasn't what hubby and I wanted. The second opportunity was in Minnesota, but that wasn't it for us, either. The third time an opportunity presented itself was in Washington. We thought about it, and at the heart of it, we wanted to move where like-minded people

were. The Pacific Northwest felt like the right place. I have a good friend in Washington; my husband has some family, and that helped with the move! Plus, we are close enough to get back to California when we need to.

What advice would you give other women in the same situation?

Look for new opportunities at work or something new in life. Always be a student of learning and growing. Squeeze the most out of life that you can. When you're at a fork in the road, be open to things you might not initially consider. The answers are there! Fear of the unknown, living in the comfort and familiar can cause you not to act. I took heat from people who thought I was crazy for leaving California. They thought moving was a bad idea. In the end, it's my life. My advice is to be honest with yourself. What do you want? What do you want to do about it? It took me a year to decide. Timing is everything, and when you decide, things happen quickly.

How did you push through?

All you can do is embrace the fear. Push through it. I love the life I have here. I'm proud that I took the chance, and I am a rule follower! Try and be brave. The older I get, I don't want to live with regret. I wasn't adventurous in my younger years. I'm in a new decade—the 50s.

What's next for you?

I haven't thought about it! We might be in the market to move to another house within Washington in order to be closer to the water. I'm thinking about going back to education.

Anything else? Parting words of wisdom?

Mortality makes its presence known as you get older. People get sick. The last thing I want is to regret not stepping outside the box. It doesn't matter what age. "Do it while you're young." That's an unfortunate mindset, looking at age as a restriction. Break that. ■

LISA STEINKAMP

Tell me a little bit about you as a child, what was it like growing up? Did you know what you wanted to be when you grew up?

I was always very creative and loved design and art. I thought I would do something creative as a job, but I was raised to be very sensible. I think it was somehow planted in my head that you do what is going to make a successful living. There were both things going on for me a little bit—being creative within the lines. I grew up in a pretty typical middle-class family in Texas and Oklahoma. I was a good student and made good grades. I think somewhere along the way, I got it in my head that advertising would be creative but could also be a respectable career. Balancing my creative side with my need for safety I guess.

When you were a child, did you have any favorite hobbies?

Yes! I was all about art and creative projects. My favorite thing to do when I was really young was to set up and decorate Barbie houses. For hours! I was obsessed with interior design and houses. Still am. I would beg my parents to let me paint my walls or put up new wallpaper. In high school, I took drafting classes and loved learning to draw floor plans.

I also liked sports and cheerleading, but being artsy was a definite theme for me. As I got older, I got interested in food and cooking, which was an underlying theme as well.

What were the college years like? Early adulthood?

I was going through the motions during the college years. I went to the University of Oklahoma because it was close and that's where my best friend was going! I think if I went back to college now, I would have studied something much closer to my true passions, like art or design. I just wasn't clear enough on it at that point.

I majored in advertising and then I was just on that path. I packed up and moved to Los Angeles without knowing a soul there, and I got an advertising job! Looking back on that, I'm amazed at the guts I had. It was something I just did without overthinking it.

Looking back in my life, those are the kind of decisions that are the right ones—the ones that just flow.

Early on, it was all new and exciting. I'd moved to LA from Oklahoma, for God's sake, which was quite a change! I was excited by all of it. I worked for an ad agency in the Marina Towers, overlooking the ocean. I remember thinking, "Oh my God, this is exactly what I was setting out to do."

I had many different marketing jobs, working with big brands like Disney, Baskin-Robbins, The Coffee Bean, and I feel like I did a good job. I was usually the most senior person at my level, and there's certain pride I felt in that. That kept me going because it felt like, "Oh, I'm doing a good job and my boss is telling me I'm doing a good job." So, it must be what I'm supposed to be doing.

Then I think you shifted into exploring something new. Can you tell us more about that?

In my late 20s, or maybe early 30s, I started to think more about what would make me happy long term. I started to feel burned out with the fast pace of marketing and advertising work, and I began a quest to find something I could do that was more independent. I read books, went to a "career intuitive" and made lists of my wants and characteristics, trying to figure out the perfect next move. Creating a product, opening a bakery or an interior design store, designing fabrics. I was kind of all over the place, but it started to become clearer and clearer that there was something I wanted to create.

After having my first child, I decided not to go back to work. Deciding to be a stay-at-home mom forced me to get out of the rut I was in at work. But being a new mom also completely rocked my world! And not always in a good way. I didn't know what to do with myself.

I immediately started thinking about what I wanted to create. I was anxious about not working but also couldn't imagine going back to work and not having the time or the flexibility I wanted with my child. I kept a notebook full of logos, brand ideas, product and company ideas that I often considered.

CHANGE YOUR THOUGHTS & YOU'LL CHANGE YOUR WORLD.

— NORMAN VINCENT PEALE

Then, we moved to Boulder, Colorado, and a few things aligned. Boulder is a foodie town and sort of a hotbed of natural food companies. That inspired me to take one of my ideas and give it a shot. I remember having a rush of energy around getting started, and I started making granola and selling it at the local farmers markets.

By the end of the first market season, I had landed a few grocery accounts too, which forced me into a real business. Commercial kitchen, better packaging, scaling production and thinking through the operations of a company, not just a product.

It's been about two and a half years since that first farmers market, and now I'm selling granola in about 12 Denver/Boulder area grocery stores and online. There haven't been any roadblocks yet, and I think it's been kind of the perfect storm of events and location. I'm not a risk taker by nature, so it has to feel pretty solid for me to take a chance and put in my all. Now, I'm at the point where I'm starting to think about getting funding to scale. There's no plan B at the moment!

What advice would you give to somebody who might be reading your story who's on the fence about pursuing an interest?

One thing I would say is to find that real core of who you are and your true interests. The thing you get lost in when you're doing it or thinking about it. That's probably the direction that will end up being fruitful for you. Find the thing that really flows for you and makes you smile when you're imagining it being successful.

What is one life experience that has shaped your character?

That's a hard one. I wouldn't say it was just one thing, but I do think that there is something about the way I was raised, that has made me feel confident and capable, and is a big part of my character. I never think that there's anything I can't do if I really made the effort.

Best or most memorable advice you've received.

An old boss of mine from Baskin-Robbins once told me, "If you make a decision and you don't like the outcome, you can make another decision to change it." I know that's such a simplistic thing, but there is power in knowing that. Nothing is permanent. You can change it.

Best book you've read or listened to lately?

There are so many. The one that I've read sort of recently that I think was great was *You Are a Badass* by Jen Sincero.

Is there anything that keeps you up at night?

On a personal level, I stress about my kids. My youngest is a handful. He's one of those kids that pushes everything to the limit!

On the subject of work, I think about, what if it doesn't work? What if people just stop buying it? I guess it ultimately boils down to fear of failing.

What is the lesson that you've had to learn over and over and over again?

Things don't have to be perfect. I know that, but it's in my nature to want to be on top of everything, just to feel balanced. I'm getting better though. I know the world will not crumble if I miss a field trip or don't get to the laundry today. ∎

@thecampfirebakery   www.thecampfirebakery.com

LIZ APPLEGATE

What was your childhood like? Did you have any favorite hobbies? Did you know what you wanted to be when you grew up?

I was probably one of the original latchkey kids. My parents divorced when I was 10. That threw me into the role of taking on adult responsibilities, where I had to start cooking for the family, picking my sister up, walking home from school. I grew up in Florida, so there was a lot of free time, a lot of climbing trees and building toad houses—I had an active imagination.

I had my own little fairy tale kind of world going on. I grew up in a time where it was very unusual for women to do sports. Title IX hadn't been passed. I wasn't very sports-minded, but I loved being outdoors: hop on the bicycle, climb trees, build tree-houses, go exploring in the forest, which we weren't allowed to do, but I did anyway.

I remember in sixth grade, we had a career day or "what do you want to be when you grow up" day. I remember struggling to come up with something. I knew that on top of being outdoors, I loved to read. I always had my nose in a book. My dad took us to the library a lot. I was reading books that the librarian didn't think I was old enough to understand.

For career day, I remember going as an author in sixth grade. I dressed up as an "author," which cracks me up now. I had a skirt on like from my mom's business suit. I had pumps on, and I wore my glasses because that's the vision that I had of how an author would look.

Now that I'm older, I realize, no, they are probably in pajamas pants most of the day. Anyway, it's kind of funny when I think back to that. In my sixth-grade mind, that's what it was.

As you got older, can you share a little bit about your career path and what did that look like?

This is an essential part of my story I need to talk about: I received an associate of science degree from a technical school instead of attending a traditional college. As I got older, I had a lot of shame around that.

I had gone to school to become a draftsman. In 1984, I started tech school and graduated in '86. By '85, I had a drafting job. That was part of the technical school set up at the time—I was able to get a job and real-life experience before graduation.

I had this vision when I started drafting that I wanted to work in retail, creating schematics for seasonal layouts and merchandising. I got offered a job doing that. But my first job in drafting was working for a place that designs sprinkler systems for commercial buildings. After having the experience of putting on a hard hat and climbing up scaffolding and seeing what I had designed, the thought of being in retail didn't give me that type of pride.

I graduated with a well-paying job, went on and got a better paying job that led me to transfer out to Dallas, Texas. I've been here ever since.

I don't do drafting anymore, but through my drafting career, it led me to learn computer-aided drafting (CAD). I learned the traditional way of drafting—standing behind a drafting table and using a ruler, mechanical pencils, and ink pens. A few years later, I was learning CAD; it was brand new to the industry. The computer was larger than my desk now! But at the time, that was the coolest thing.

Because that was such a new technology, it opened a lot of doors for me. This gave me the confidence to realize that I could learn new technology. And back then, technology wasn't in our "everyday world" the way it is now.

So, you've got experience with computers. What else?

Fast forward to 1992, I stayed home after my first son was born, for a year. I thought I wanted to be a stay-at-home mom, but I didn't really do well as a stay-at-home mom. I love my children dearly, but I needed something to mentally stimulate myself. I wasn't getting it. So, I did end up going back to work. I went back to drafting, but eventually, after three kids, I couldn't do that.

Desktop publishing had just started at this point, and I realized, "Oh, I can teach myself!" I used to create family letters and cards. It's so crazy to think

Midlife is when the UNIVERSE gently places her hands upon your shoulders, pulls you close, and whispers in your ear ... it's time to show up & be seen.

—BRENÉ BROWN

about how cheesy desktop publishing was then. But I taught myself, with the confidence that I gained through my drafting career.

That led to a new career, going into marketing and communications. When my kids were independent, I began working for nonprofits and faith-based organizations. And the thread of this all started with my first drafting job of me drawing sprinkler systems or designing water treatment plants.

I think we need to remind ourselves of this now at this time of life. Something can spark an interest or you realize that you are good at something, and it may be totally unexpected. Follow that path and see where that leads because you just never know. So, anyway, that's my story.

What else would you like to share about your life's journey?

I ended up divorced at age 39, and I started looking at my life. I began asking, "Is this really what I want to do for the rest of my life?" I was ready to make big changes, and through all that, I hired a life coach. I have to say, it was a disappointment. I understood the support that I wanted and needed, and I thought that I could do a better job supporting others than my coach had done for me. So, again, following that path of what I needed at the time and then creating a new skill, I began my training to become a certified life coach.

In the meantime, because of my work with nonprofits, where you basically have to do everything yourself, online marketing was exploding onto the scene, and I was teaching myself that. I was being asked to help other businesses with their online marketing. I was asked to lead training workshops.

And I did all that for free for a long time until I realized that I did not want to work for someone else for the rest of my life. I decided to start charging for my services and launch a side business.

I had a virtual assistant/online business management company for about four years. I had also become a life coach to help my virtual assistant/online business management clients, and I had fallen in love

with coaching and decided to shift my business in that direction.

And then, I had two kids in college, and with trying to help them, I was tired of stressing about money. I took the easy way out and decided to go back to a 9-to-5 job. I don't know if it was the right decision, but that was the decision at the time. I do think the shift in my business created a lot of fear, so it was logical to return to a full-time job. Looking back, I still feel I had to go through that. I had to learn those lessons. It made me look at my patterns and how I keep "playing small." I realized that I need to buckle down and do what I need to do.

In all of this, you started a podcast. Midlife Schmidlife. How did that come about?

I did! I was approaching 50, and it freaked me out. It's the first time that age has really ever gotten to me. But as I was approaching 50, I definitely knew, OK, shit, I'm hitting midlife.

Looking back, I have no idea why, but I Googled "midlife," and the definition that came up was "the wrong side of 40," and I was like, "Fuck that, fuck that!" I mean, honestly!

I used humor a lot to kind of get me through things, and I was like, "Oh, fuck that, midlife schmidlife!" and that kind of stuck with me. Then, I had this vision that I'd wanted to start a podcast. That gave me the platform of what to talk about.

What's the life experience that had shaped your character?

Oh, there's so many. I can't think of one that hasn't, honestly.

Whether it's been the career choices or divorce or having children, probably having children is perhaps the one that I can say significantly, big time. Not that most women wouldn't say that, but that made me grow up and made me feel like I had a purpose. I don't know that I felt like I had that before. That would probably be the one with the most effect.

Some memorable advice that you've received that has stuck with you over the years?

I had a teacher in high school who influenced me

and gave me motherly energy. She saw something in me. I don't feel like I ever had anyone else give that to me in that way. She made me see something in myself, too. I knew that I wanted to help others see the best in themselves, as well.

Oh, that's great. What's an inspiring book that you've read lately?

I wrote a chapter for this book called *Mokita: How to Navigate Perimenopause With Confidence & Ease* by Shirley Weir. It was written by 13 professionals, and I wrote Chapter 9.

Mokita is a word that actually means the elephant in the room. It's something that is there that we don't want to talk about. It talks about building a health care team when you're heading into the middle years of life and experiencing perimenopause instead of just taking the typical, "Oh, you're getting older, you just need to get over it," kind of attitude.

When daughters are going through puberty, moms will read up on how to help them and what words to say and find the right doctor, but as we're getting older and we're approaching a new stage of life, we need to do our research and take care of our health. We don't have an illness; menopause is not a disease. That would be the book I would recommend.

What is the lesson you've had to learn over and over again?

Oh, everything, every single thing. Stay the course, or maintenance is always easier than having to restart over. This is true with your health, or your finances, or your relationships.

Any type of relationship in your life, whether it's money or food or exercise or friendships or marriage...maintenance, and putting that amount of effort into that, is so much easier than having to start over or to restart. Maybe it's not even starting over but re-energizing. I think that that is a lesson that I'm continually being reminded of.

What if anything keeps you up at night?

Besides my low progesterone levels? Besides worrying about my children? The state of the world right now makes me very sad and very concerned

What message would you like to give to our readers who are in their middle years, wondering what's next, or is it too late to pursue my dreams? What would you like to tell them?

I would say that it's only too late if you think it's too late. We're continually being reminded of people that didn't start things until later in life.

We are in such a wonderful time in history, speaking of technology. We can learn to do anything. If you have a passion for photography, you can learn photography from anywhere in the world by taking a course online at CreativeLive. There's YouTube. There's Google. There are online communities that you can get involved with. There are things in your community that you can get involved with.

I feel like we are in such a time of greatness that we don't have to just settle. You don't have to say, "Well, this is what I am. This is all I know, so this is what I am."

Honestly, I get a little bit on my soapbox about this because I can't stand when people say things like, "I'm not good with the computer, I'm not good at technology." Good grief, you don't have to be. You have to have a little bit of patience with yourself or ask someone else to help you. Take a freaking computer class at the library. If you want to stay stuck in that belief, then you can't complain. If you believe that, you're going to stay stuck in that kind of narrative. But if you want to get out of it, I'm here to help. If that's the place where you are, then you're only limited by what you think you can or what you can't do. ∎

www.elizabethapplegate.com

LIZ ZIEGLER

What was it like growing up for you? Did you know what you wanted to be when you grew up?

I grew up in Pleasanton, which is a suburb in the Bay Area. Pleasanton is pretty big now, but when I was young it wasn't too big of a town. And it was nice, it was safe, good schools, a great area in terms of being near cool stuff, but there wasn't really anything going on right in town. Looking back on it, I appreciate it, and I was fortunate to grow up there. Like many kids, I also could not wait to get out and see something new.

I was a good kid. I got pretty good grades in school, nothing earth-shattering. I grew up thinking that you graduate high school, you go to college and then you have some great career.

For a long time, I wanted to be a teacher, up until about high school age when you're kind of getting to the difficult rebellious teenage years. My parents went to work in an office, but I had no clue what they did! It was all very nebulous!

There was no real deep thinking about "well, what exactly do I want to do?" The teacher idea came and went. It was more that I knew what the next step was going to be, so I just had to do that. That's what happened. I graduated high school applied to schools, and got into all except the one that I really wanted to go to, which was UC-Berkeley.

Where did you land? What did you end up taking?

I ended up going to UCLA, having no clue what I was going to major in and with no big ambition.

When I started at UCLA, I loved it. I was so glad to be somewhere different, somewhere where they didn't roll up the streets at 10 p.m. There's always something to do, and I was meeting so many new people. I thought, "Yes, this is where I should be."

I kind of fumbled for a couple of years. Initially, I thought maybe I'd major in French because that was my favorite subject when I was in high school. I did take a few French classes, and it just started feeling like, "OK, if you're going to major in this, you'd better really love it." I didn't have the drive for it. Then I took

just one intro to political science class, and I loved it, so I ended up majoring in political science. My parents had always been very politically minded, so I started thinking maybe I'd want to pursue something related to government.

I ended up graduating with a political science degree. It took me a little more than four years, and I did work a little bit during school. I did a summer internship in Washington, D.C., working for the Democratic National Committee, which was a highlight.

Starting in my fourth year of college, I got a job as an unpaid intern at a really small nonprofit called Kidsave. It was brand new, a startup. I worked out of the boss' garage. It was very grassroots. We raised money and organized a program that would bring older kids who live in overseas orphanages to the United States for summer camp. While they were here, they were hosted by families and met other families who were interested in adoption. We found that when the families could meet the kids and get to know them, a love connection would often happen, and the families would decide to adopt.

It was a rare opportunity because I was super young. I was so green, and they gave me a lot of responsibility because the staff was so small. I think I was 20 when I started there. I was in meetings and talking with families and doing very hands-on work. Then they transitioned me to a small hourly wage, and when I graduated, they put me on salary, and hired me full time. I was their West Coast program coordinator for the summer visit program.

The work itself was rewarding because we got to meet the kids and the families and see the results of all our efforts. I learned so much, but the work was hard and so stressful. The stakes felt very high because they were. This was before cellphones were common, and all the families, translators and volunteers would have my home phone number, so even at home, I was never off the clock. I was always working.

What happened next?

What do you do when you're that age and already feeling burned out? You go to law school! So cliche!

Without really thinking it through, one day, I decided I was going to take the LSAT. I figured I'm just going to sign up, I'm going to pay the money, I'm going to study, and I'm going to just see what happens. I never thought beyond that. A few months later, I took the LSAT, and I did pretty well, not amazing but well enough where I thought, "Okay, I'll probably get in somewhere."

I got into Tulane in New Orleans. I gave my notice at the job and then spent most of the money that I had saved up on the move. I gave up the apartment that I loved in West Hollywood and went to New Orleans where I knew nobody. I remember feeling at the orientation like I did not belong there. I did my first year in law school, there and before the next semester started, I was thinking "Oh, God. Oh my God, what am I doing?" I was having panic and anxiety issues, and thinking how am I going to get through this? Looking back, I knew right away that it was a mistake, but I felt committed and had already given up so much to be there.

But you powered through?

Yeah, I did. I talked to my faculty advisor, who happened to be the dean of the school. I broke down in her office one day during the first semester and told her, "I don't know if I should be here, but I've spent all my money. Now I'm stuck in New Orleans." The dean told me I was supposed to feel like this. It's a big change from how school usually is. She said that their goal is to completely change the way you think and analyze situations, so it's supposed to be a jarring adjustment. That did make me feel a little better, so I decided to keep plugging along.

But I was so nervous every single day there. I studied so hard because I always felt underprepared. I would read assignments multiple times and take tons of notes because I never wanted to feel unprepared in class. But no matter how much I did, I always felt like I was behind everyone else. I am not good at the "fake it 'til you make it" thing! But I ended up getting good-enough grades to transfer back to UCLA for my second year. During your second year,

all the big firms come to the big schools, and they do on-campus 15-minute interviews with the students. It's like a legal profession cattle call. I went through all these interviews with all these different firms, and it was just not feeling right. I kept thinking, this is just wrong. What am I doing? None of this fits me at all!

I did end up getting an offer to work in the summer at one of the big firms downtown. This is called a summer associate position, and it's kind of the firm's chance to try you out to see if they want to hire you after you graduate. I took the summer job because they offered it, and it's just what is expected of you if you are at a big law school. They paid more than I ever imagined I would make. They wine and dine you, and try to make it seem like working at the firm is really great. But for me, it was so bad. I knew that I was not fit for that kind of job. The partner would say, "I'm going to take all the summer associates out tonight to whatever fancy, expensive restaurant." As if it were some big treat. And all I could think was, "Ugh, I just want to go home! I don't want to be around these people anymore." Everyone else seemed so into it, but all I could think was "This is my nightmare!"

Then what?

At the end of the summer, this firm decides which associates they want to hire for a postgraduate position. The whole summer is geared toward "Who is going to get the offers?" It has a game-show feel to it. I got an offer. And I took it because that's what I was supposed to do. It was what I was supposed to want.

I graduated. I had the job lined up. I studied for the bar, which is a nightmare. I passed the bar in the first try, thank goodness because I would not have wanted to go through that again. When I got my exam results, I wasn't happy though. It was a realization that I had to now actually be a lawyer! There was no putting it off. I felt stuck and trapped.

So, I'm working at this firm, and I don't even last a year there. I was commuting by train from Hollywood to downtown, and I would cry on the train every morning. I remember I would always bring a book with me because I could hold the book up over my

A coward dies a thousand times before his death but the valiant taste of death but once.

— WILLIAM SHAKESPEARE

face and try to hide from everyone sitting near me on the train. During one especially bad week when my parents just happened to be in town, something happened at work that set me off, which happened pretty much daily. I called my dad because I knew he was in town and said, "I can't keep doing this. I don't know what I'm going to do." He told me, "I think you should quit." It felt like I had permission. I went home sick that day and came back the next day to give my notice. The firm was pretty much like, "OK, just leave." They didn't even have me stay through my notice period, which was fine with me!

Where did you go from there?

I bounced around doing temp legal work for eight—yes, eight—years. I signed up with different legal staffing agencies, and they would place me at different big firms around town. The jobs varied in length: A few were just a few months or a few weeks; some were a few years—but it was never steady. You always knew it could end at any moment since they were temporary assignments, and I never knew where my next job was going to be. But it was my time to slow down and recover.

I spent pretty much the whole eight years thinking about what else I could do, tormenting myself with lists, pros and cons, making budgets, scrolling through job listings, praying it would come to me in a flash. It never did, but I knew what I didn't want. I didn't want to sit at a desk anymore; I didn't want to be at the computer all day; I didn't want a rigid life anymore. I definitely didn't want to be a lawyer. I would love to be my own boss.

I remember saying to people that the way I'm going to be happy is if I'm around animals all day. They would kind of roll their eyes, like "OK, you want to play with puppies all day for your job? Good luck with that."

Sounds like an epiphany?

It took me a long time to even say it out loud because it just seemed so pie-in-the-sky and kind of silly. I had a law degree and what I was considering was basically the polar opposite of that!

Where did that come from? Was that something where, as a child, you had pets or liked to be around animals?

Yeah, definitely. We always had cats. We never had dogs, but we always had a lot of cats. My cat Lewis was my best friend when I was growing up. As I got older, I got more into animal rights and animal rescue stuff. In eighth grade, I stopped eating meat after watching the movie *City Slickers* because I felt very connected to the cow in the movie-Norman. Norman changed my life! I became vegan after law school. Animal rights was always a growing theme in my life.

When I started telling people that I was thinking of switching careers to something that would allow me to be around animals, they would almost always say, "Well, why don't you try to get a law job at an animal-rights group, something where you're a lawyer but you're doing it for animals." And I was like, "No! I want to be around the animals! Not taking depositions about them." I know that animal rights attorneys do a lot of heavy-duty litigation work, and I never wanted to do courtroom work. I knew that would not suit me at all.

What came up next?

I started thinking about a dog grooming business. I started researching it to see if you could actually make a living at it, and how do you even start? Finally, after mulling this idea over for a few months, I left the law job I was at. I took about a month off to do absolutely nothing but try to put myself back together, and then I called up a local dog grooming school and asked, "Can I come to see your facility?" I signed up on the spot.

I went through the grooming school, and it was really hard! There's a major learning curve, and it was like nothing else I had ever tried to learn and master before. There were many times I wondered how I could ever accomplish this? Some of the tasks seemed impossible. The advice from the school was practice, practice, practice, practice. Then, practice more! So, I did.

The schooling was only supposed to be a certain

number of hours. I still didn't feel ready after I hit the hours, so I kept coming back. I did a lot of extra training, then the school hired me to work there. They have a mobile service that they offered clients, and they hired me to work in that.

I did that for a little while. The grooming part was great, but working for someone else again was not so great. I kept reminding myself, "I now know I can do the work. But I want to be on my own, in control of my schedule, the pricing, I'll be in charge of all of it." I left there and bought a truck and started my business.

Fantastic! How's business going?

Really good. It took about six months before it was like, "OK, at least I'm making some money." It took about a year before I was like, "OK, this is good, I'm comfortable." Now, a few years in, it's exactly where I had hoped it would be. I have my steady clients. They're my bread and butter. They're 90% of my business. Now and then, I'll add a new person in, but now I can be picky about who I take. Since the dogs are all familiar to me now, I know what to expect. There's no stress to it; the days are just really nice. I like being in the truck and with the dogs. Just me and the dogs, and I put on my podcast or my music, and it's like my little sanctuary. And the dogs don't get annoyed when I sing to them!

Thanks for sharing your story. My next question is: What life experience shaped your character?

When I was in college, probably like my third year or so, I started having panic attacks. The first time it happened, I was sitting in a small seminar class, around a table with other students and the professor. Participating in class had never been a problem for me before, and in fact, I was often that annoying student who raised her hand at every question! But this day, the professor asked me a question, and I didn't know the answer, and couldn't get anything coherent out of my mouth. The panic just completely set in, and I had an attack in front of the whole class. I remember thinking, "Am I losing my mind? Am I having a heart attack? What's going on?"

That began a series of such experiences over the years. It changes your outlook on things. It was a big battle dealing with that during law school when most of the classes are modeled on the Socratic method, and on any given day, you will be called upon to answer a series of questions in front of the class. I basically spent three years dripping in anxiety, and it was exhausting. But it made me work extra hard, and I learned to take a lot of pride in setting a goal and meeting it. I also think that having a history of dealing with panic and anxiety makes you a more compassionate person. You pick up on cues of how others are feeling, and you know when they are uncomfortable, and you can try to make them more at ease.

What's the best advice that you've received?

I had just started my business and things were going wrong. When I bought my truck, it had all these mechanical problems. I was spending so much money to get the thing running, even though I was not making any money yet. I remember complaining to a friend and saying, "I don't know, I think maybe this isn't going to work. I might have to get another law job." She texted me back, "Be brave," and that was it. Now whenever I feel like I don't know if I can get through something, I remind myself, "Be brave. Do it. Be brave."

If you're taking a risk, you have to be a little brave. Doing something that's not the "normal" path seems to be a little brave in and of itself. It can be scary, and you don't have to be fearless, but you do have to face the fear.

What's the best book you've read?

I read a ton. I go through like almost a book a week. Like everyone who went to law school, I read *To Kill a Mockingbird* and that one did have an impact on me.

I read the book *Shrill* by Lindy West. She had a column in *The New York Times* for a while. I read *Shrill* in late 2016, and it was just exactly what I needed at that moment in time.

A lesson you have to learn over and over again?

A hard lesson to learn, especially when you have your own business and you work by yourself, is to trust your gut and to trust yourself. It took me a long time. When you first start your business, you'll take anyone who comes your way. "I'll go anywhere, whatever price, just hire me please."

It took me a while to pick up on the red flags. For instance, I got a call from someone who said, "My dog has been to 10 different groomers, and they're all awful." Hmm… But I went anyway. It was a disaster, of course, because I'm not magic and neither were the other groomers; this dog needed to be groomed by a vet because it wasn't well-behaved.

I finally learned to trust my instincts and say "no." "This is just not worth it. Let them go somewhere else. Let it go. It's not worth the stress." Trust yourself: "I can do it. Be brave."

What message would you like to impart to our readers who might feel stuck as you did in law school?

When you know you have to do something, but you're just not sure it's the right time or if you have enough money saved, you have to find the balance between planning and taking action. I don't think acting on a whim is the way to go. Yes, you may hate your job, but the reality is, you do need to do a little planning before making the leap. Do your budget. Save a little cushion. Do some research about the next steps. Because doing all this planning is what is going to give you the confidence to take the leap and to keep going when challenges pop up. But at the same time, you don't want to overplan and psych yourself out. You'll never have enough money saved, and the timing will never be 100% perfect, so eventually, you do just have to do it.

Decide on a timeline and stick to it. Also, remember nothing is final. If my business folds tomorrow, I still have my degree. I can go back to the agencies and figure out what's next if I had to. We can make the stakes seem so high for every decision, but we have to remember that we can do a little bit of experimenting without it meaning it will be a lifelong change. ∎

@Must Love Dogs Mobile   MustLoveDogsMobileGrooming

MEGAN SULLIVAN

Could you tell me a little bit about what it was like for you as a child; did you know what you wanted to be when you grew up?

It's so interesting when you start to reflect on childhood. I oftentimes feel like as we get older, it's kind of coming back to yourself. My main impression of being young is spending a lot of happy time alone playing in my room, just lost in thought in my head. No one would describe me like that; I'm a very social person—my grandma used to say I had "personality plus,"—yet I always had a very active inner world and was observant of the world and people around me. As early as I can remember, I have studied people.

I'm a middle child and the only girl in my Midwestern family. I was very curious and kind of risky also, I was a rule tester. I remember spying and writing down what my brothers were doing, but I was also a stereotypical middle child in some respects—a little bit brooding. I felt misunderstood. And part of that was due to not having an immediate female role model that I related to. My mom, I love her, but we're very different. I think I related more to males and tried to mimic them, but I also felt like that wasn't quite right. I remember wearing fake glasses and bending a paper clip and putting it in my mouth so it looked like I wore a retainer. I wanted to stand out in some way, find my place in things.

Did you have any particular hobbies that you gravitated to?

I'm a generalist, a dabbler. Curious about everything and prefer breadth over depth. I am still like this—I like to cast a wide net and skim the world for information. I lose interest quickly. I have always liked to push myself physically as well, so I loved sports. I observed people a good deal of the time—I was fascinated by human behavior.

What about the transition from the teen years to becoming a young adult and starting your career? How did that look for you?

It was tough. There was very little guidance around career. I majored in psychology. I was always interested in human dynamics. I also did peer counseling in college. Then it was sort of like, what do I from here? I do also traveled abroad, and I still couldn't really, in my immature mind, distill what this life was meant to be.

My first real job was working in a psych hospital. Because I had majored in psychology, and as a 22-year-old who was pretty much clueless about the depths of real struggle, I ended up working as a psych tech in an inpatient suicidal/homicidal unit. It was a private hospital with the most misogynist, backward owner who was trying to profit off the revolving door of patients. He made all the female employees wear skirts. If you're dealing with someone who is detoxing from heroin, they will fight you to the death for meds—there was physical violence there. And I am wearing a skirt—it's restrictive and symbolic of these gender norms. It was a highly toxic environment. Every day, I just left there overwhelmed. It paid nothing. I was working in bars and restaurants at night just to make ends meet. It broke me because it was a dual diagnosis unit. There were so many elements that now in my mid-40s, I understand. There was addiction and recidivism, and as a naïve 22-year-old, I was so optimistic! I was eager to help, and it was a whole new depth of human suffering that I had never experienced before.

I remember one woman, a soccer mom. Three out of her four siblings, as well as her mom and her grandma, committed suicide—inherited suicidal tendencies. It was a struggle for her every day just to stay alive. I left there broken because I couldn't quickly help people. I had thought that if I came in with the best intentions, that I could really make an impact. In that environment, I did not feel I could make any difference.

It was so humbling and also a pivotal experience for me. Looking back, this had a profound impact on my ability to meet people where they are at and be of greater service.

What happened after that job?

I thought, "OK, I guess, it's not psychology for me, what is it that I like? What is it about psychology that I love?" I realized that it was conflict resolution. At that moment, I decided to go to grad school. I moved to Washington, D.C., and studied international peace and conflict resolution.

It was kind of a confusing period. If I could chalk up my 20s to anything, it would be a good deal of personal suffering and some level of real interpersonal growth. So here I am at grad school saying, "OK, I want to do this," and then, kind of being bored and uninspired at the same time there.

I didn't want to graduate and end up making no money just to be part of the "right" organization. That's how I was feeling about all of it. I dropped out of grad school. It didn't feel right, and I wasn't going to finish just for the sake of finishing it—that's been a recurring thing for me.

So, I worked at a startup, and I felt my brain wasn't being used—no one was seeing my strengths and capabilities. I was broke. I was temping as an office manager, and the woman who started the company was this rich, overprivileged woman—she would put her bare feet on her desk with her fresh pedicure.

I would order office supplies and do other stuff. She came over to me one day with her coffee cup, making an exaggerated sad face, and she said, "Megan, can you please make me coffee, nobody makes it as good as you do." It was such a defining moment for me around self-worth—this backhanded compliment. That story stays with me because it was such a perfect example of privilege and ignorance.

I did not want to work in the corporate world, but I was floundering. Somehow, I was able to get a job at Accenture even though my resume was not at all impressive—I was not one of those people that did an internship in college. I always had to hustle and make money. So, I started working for corporate America as a consultant and stayed there for 13 years.

What did you do at Accenture?

What I learned was that in most jobs, the stuff that was interesting and fun for me was extracurricular and not part of my day-to-day job there.

What was the stuff that you found interesting while you are working there?

I was in customer relationship management, focused on the customer and employee experience, and this is what was ultimately interesting to me. That kind of work—helping people stay engaged, whether it's helping humans stay engaged in jobs or how you create a helpful experience for customers. The industry work that I found most compelling was doing government work. After 9/11, I was put on a project that eventually became New York City's information phone number—311. It was an interesting challenge—how do you create an accessible government for citizens, and what do they care about? How do you bring government closer to them? Making an impact like that was the best of the best. I eventually moved to an internal research and development role when I started a family. I love research and writing, so it provided an outlet for that as well. I was able to get published in that way with Accenture. I liked to have a couple of different projects going at the same time.

After Accenture, what was next for you?

It was a pivotal time for me because I knew that for over 13 years, I had run businesses. At that point, I was very senior. I was running, selling, designing and managing projects. I was over the pulsating stress of consulting work, travel, etc.

I've gotten married; I have my kids. I made it work for me. In the last couple of years, I've been working from home in more of a research and development role—that's been great. I love mentoring and coaching. I feel like I've never been a great manager—but now, managing is more like ongoing coaching, so I know I'm there. I will say, people love to be on my teams, and people always feel inspired. There was something that was second nature to me about coaching and championing people. I finally had this realization that just because I am good at something does not mean I'm meant to do it forever.

I had a conversation with my husband and asked him to support me in quitting this job, which meant

SUCCESS IS GOING
FROM FAILURE TO
FAILURE without
LOSING ENTHUSIASM

- WINSTON
CHURCHILL

that not only was our household income going to be cut in half, but I would also have to spend money to get certified as a coach. There's no knowable time frame of when I'll be making money again, but he has this belief in me. I know he was nervous, but ultimately he believed in me, and so that's what started me on a coaching journey.

That's wonderful! Where are you on this new journey?

The marketing, the self-selling, it's just not my forte, but I am learning. With individual coaching, it's all referrals. I do a lot of refreshing of my website and stuff like that, but I just can't be too bothered.

Over time, I missed the creative journey. After two or three years, I was re-inspired. Another pivotal point for me was seeing Fred Rogers—I don't know if you've ever seen this—in his 1969 appeal to the Senate for funding for public television.

He had such a strong mission statement for what he wanted to offer children. Watching that show stirred something inside me—it made me think about how to create an environment where I am in that inspirational zone. This is what we need in organizations. All the engagement stuff that I did in the private sector, in the corporate sector, I thought, we're missing the mark. I've seen this in psych hospitals; we're missing what it is that humans want in the workplace that keep them there.

This led to a one-year journey to create my company KNOCK. The idea behind it is, what could it look like if we had neighborhood-like cultures at work, where everyone felt a sense of purpose and collective wellness that integrates the critical ideas of engagement, inclusion and diversity?

Who do you leave your career "keys" to when you are out of town? What's the workplace equivalent of a neighborhood block party or a potluck? How do we create a sense of care? That led to this whole creative journey for me with a partner that I met through a certification program. We built this thing for a year and put a bunch of money into it, formed the LLC, etc. I really wanted a partnership, but it's a tough

journey filled with rejection, and my partner wanted to be done sooner than I did. I ended up working in total isolation and selling projects on my own. It made me miserable, even though I wholeheartedly believe in the concept. I shut the doors in order to move forward. When I allow things to linger in uncertainty is when I'm the most miserable.

There's a difference between when you're lingering and when you have a gut feeling of what to do and you're not doing it. It's the period of uncertainty where you are in it and it's unknown versus when you know what to do and you don't do it. You don't want to activate the courage to do it; it's a miserable feeling. For me, this meant dissolving the LLC and moving forward into a new unchartered version of the future. Closing that door opened up incredible opportunities, not the least of which was the opportunity to fulfill a lifelong dream and move to New Zealand!

We moved in January 2019 and started this incredible journey—complete with yet another opportunity to build a new career path here—which has been scary and exhilarating at the same time. At this point, I'm involved in all the work activities I want to be doing in terms of coaching, facilitation and creating powerful and interesting experiences for different clients. My main motivation and focus is around whole-person well-being. I'm on a mission to make sure that all the hours that we spend away from our families, our communities and people we love are ones that we don't reflect on with regret, but instead are ones that contribute to our personal growth and our best life journey.

What's next for you and your family?

What does the future hold? What we want it to! I've developed a resilient skin and feel proud we made this leap. I am honoring my deepest values of adventure and learning for myself and my family and trying new things all the time. Professionally, I am looking to get more deeply involved in work in our new country to make a difference here. I am taking my time to find the right outlet, and in the meantime, I am working with clients and partnerships in seven countries! As a family, we want to continue to embrace the slower pace here, to adapt and adjust to our new life. Anyone can work 70 hours a week—my challenge will always be working less in favor of a more fulfilling life. I am convinced I can have it all—good money, great work and tons of free time. Why not choose to believe that? Stay tuned!

Great. We'll leave it at that. You've given me a lot of moments, but my next question is, is there a life experience that has really shaped your character?

Breakups and shake-ups throughout my life have really made an impact. I seek out opportunities to shake up my life in order to create impact. Studying abroad/traveling, switching careers, having children—these are huge moments that deliver with them opportunities for tremendous growth. I like to think that I have seized these transformative opportunities and that my current wonderful adventurous and fulfilling life is proof.

What's the best or most memorable advice you've received?

I have two pieces of advice. One is—and I love this, I tell clients this all the time—other people's opinions of me are none of my business. The second one came from one of my mentors. She said, "At all costs don't create cosmic waste. Make sure everything can be reused, recycled." I think about that when it relates to my actions, my words—don't create cosmic waste. Gossip, entrenched negativity, self/other judgments—this is all cosmic waste that weighs heavy in the atmosphere. I aim to create lightness, levity, unburdening.

Do you have a favorite book, or is there just one that stands out to you?

Jesmyn Ward's *Sing, Unburied, Sing*. She's just a phenomenal writer, and I cried for 30 minutes after finishing this book. I cried at the unfair ways of the world and the suffering that exists. I appreciate books that teach me about something real in society wrapped in beautiful fiction writing.

A lesson you have had to learn over and over again?

Are you familiar with *The Four Agreements*? Be impeccable with your word. Don't make assumptions. Always do your best. And don't take anything personally. These are the lessons that I keep working on—I have a picture of *The Four Agreements* everywhere I turn. They are simple and yet profoundly powerful. Another lesson is, nothing anyone ever does or says is because of you.

And a message you would like to impart to the readers of this book who are in their 40s or beyond, or anybody who picks up the book. If they're on the fence about trying something new or going for something they're passionate about, what advice would you give them?

I would say, know what the message is that you tell yourself that keeps you from doing that thing—let's say pursuing something new. I know it sounds counter-intuitive, but I would say to follow that message, and if it leads you to do nothing, then that voice is holding you back. If it leads you to do nothing, then you know it's a lie. Don't ignore it. Give it space for a moment and follow it. Perfection is the enemy of progress. ■

www.meganconnorsullivan.com   www.knock.world

MICHELLE CAMAYA JULIAN

Could you tell me a little bit about what it was like for you as a child?

In a nutshell, I come from parents who immigrated to the United States from the Philippines. My parents met while my dad was in the Navy and my mom was in California visiting her sister, whose husband was also in the Navy. My pops traveled frequently due to work, so much of my upbringing was through my mother's guidance. I have two older brothers, and my parents divorced when I was 13 years old. My mom enrolled me in dance classes at the early age of 4, and I've been dancing ever since.

And is that what you wanted to be when you grew up? A dancer?

There was no time to ask that question. I was already quite active in tap dance, ballet, Tae Kwon Do, swimming, Philippine folk dance, jazz, ballroom, modern, hula, Tahitian, theater arts, and youth dance companies; I even had a ballroom partner—John Selby—at the age of 13. In regards to choosing and thinking about what I wanted to be when I grew up, my path was already laid out for me. To be honest, this brought up much reflection in my later years because I would contemplate what my life would be like if I had been given the chance to choose.

I remember when I was a young teenager, maybe 12 or 13 years old, I argued with my mom. I wanted to take a break from dancing for a year, and she said, "Would you rather spend your time working at McDonald's?" I thought I was spending all my childhood years cooped up in dance classes, but in fact, it all guided me to my career. All the time I was dedicated to dance classes paved a way for my life as a performing artist. I've had an incredible career performing and never had any type of job besides teaching dance, teaching yoga and being a professional performing artist. My mom had the best of intentions for me, and I am truly grateful for that.

Did you enjoy some of it more than others? It seems like the full spectrum of all kinds of performance arts.

A lot of the dancing that I trained in was very technical—ballet, modern, ballroom dancing and theater arts. It wasn't until I went to college at UC Irvine that I became interested in urban dancing styles, more of my generation in the 1990s. I was a member of a hip-hop crew called Kaba Modern, which was connected to the Filipino club on campus, Kababayan. In 2008, the crew became popular from the MTV show *America's Best Dance Crew* (season 1). Training for years in ballet, modern and jazz, and then learning this entirely new style of dance actually felt natural in my body. I will always love partner dancing because I love being able to let go and be the follow while someone else takes the lead—it's exhilarating!

Dance was your life and so that was your career? So how did that work?

As a teenager, I frequently performed in the San Diego community, for family celebrations, anniversaries, weddings, birthday parties and charity events. While I was in college, majoring in dance, I got representation from a dance agent and drove countless miles from Irvine to Los Angeles to attend all types of auditions. I booked many kinds of job—from short-lived gigs like music videos to bigger-budgeted productions like touring musicals, which had me traveling all around the world. The big gig that changed the trajectory of my life was in 1998, when I booked the first national tour of *Fame*, the musical. I decided to drop out of school right before my senior year at UC Irvine to take the opportunity to tour the country for two years. In 2001, I booked another big gig and toured the country for nine months with *Swing*, the musical. Then in 2002, I was cast in the first national tour of *The Lion King*. This show has been the most impactful in my life and has enabled me to perform in the Broadway and Las Vegas productions. I'm proud to share that I've performed in *The Lion King* over 2,500 times throughout 17 years.

Was it fun or was it like, ugh, I'm on the road all the time?

The full spectrum! Imagine—I was 21 years old and had booked a job that brought me to New York to rehearse and then tour the country doing what I loved to do...while getting paid! That's what I call a dream come true. I was able to join the Actors' Equity Association, the labor union representing American actors and stage managers in theater. Every city we went to, I searched out shopping malls. It was all about shopping, shopping, shopping for me back then. I was living what I thought to be my best life, until I came back home to San Diego, and my mom handed me a stack of money. She said, "Now, throw it in the air!" So I did. I threw all the money in the air, and she said, "Guess what, that is all the money that you've saved so far. It can go at any time." She thought that I was spending frivolously on the road and had to make a point by demonstrating to me how money can easily come and go. She taught me that I was not always going to make this amount of money in my life but would always need to spend money throughout my life. She further explained, "While you're making money, save it!" That changed my whole perspective and work ethic. For the rest of my time on tour, I made it a priority to save and invest my money.

CHOOSE L♥VE

— MICHELLE
CAMAYA
JULIAN

Moms have a way of teaching us, don't they? What are you up to now?

My husband and I moved into a beautiful new home. We live close to his parents, Momma Del and Papa Ray—we're very close with them. They're in their 70s, and we love them dearly. They spoil us with their delicious cooking. I'm looking at my dry erase board right now and can see that I'm in the middle of multiple projects. I have a business called Kamochi Method with my passion partner and friend, Karine Plantadit. We offer dance intensive programs for young artists, and we host yoga retreats to adventurous places. Right now, we're preparing for a yoga retreat in Guadeloupe in the French West Indies. Karine is French African and has familial roots in that area. I've been involved with the Philippine folk dance company Samahan Filipino American Performing Arts & Education Center since the age of 8, and am now a dance teacher and co-choreographer for the 45-year-old nonprofit organization, founded by my mentor, the late Dr. Lolita Carter. I was recently asked to substitute teach for dance classes at a high school, while the dance teacher, Christine Timmons, was on maternity leave. Excited for this opportunity, I applied, studied and tested to be in the Sweetwater Unified School District. It's a very thorough and in-depth process to be in the school system, so I prepared and thankfully passed all the exams. I graduated from the San Diego School of Creative and Performing Arts in 1995. For SDSCPA's 40th anniversary this year, they invited me to be a guest choreographer for their spring concert titled Reflecting Forward. I'm setting an all-female dance piece to Aretha Franklin's "Amazing Grace." The dance is dedicated to my late mother, Violeta Aguilar—and to all mothers and daughters. My mom sang that song almost every day to her grandson, Nicasio. On top of all this, I passionately guide people in hot hatha yoga practice and Inferno Hot Pilates.

Wow, you've got a whole bunch of different things going on! It all sounds enriching and fun. My next question is: Is there a life experience that shaped your character?

Being a part of the professional theater world for over 20 years has shaped me tremendously. Working with high-caliber artists and being surrounded by talented actors, dancers, singers, musicians, directors, producers and management teams has taught me so much about professionalism, collaboration and hard work, and has given me confidence in myself. Before I left New York and moved back to San Diego, I was offered a temporary position to return to *The Lion King* touring company. While the show was in San Antonio, and as I was at the end of fulfilling my contract, my mom had a bad fall. A dear friend and former dance teacher, Mary Murphy, called late on a Saturday night to inform me that my mom was in intensive care from hitting her head falling down some stairs. I took the next flight out to San Diego. My mom was on life support for four days. My two brothers no longer lived in San Diego, so Raymond, whom I was dating at the time (now my husband), was the first one I called, and he arrived immediately at my mother's side. My brother, Jay, drove down from Orange County with his family, and our oldest brother, Jo, flew in from the Philippines a day later with his pregnant wife Klara, their son Nicasio, our first cousin Sheila and her mom, Auntie Tess—our mom's beloved older sister. This was a heartbreaking and shattering time for all of us.

Four days later, when it came time for the doctor to ask us what we wanted to do, we decided to take our mom off of life support and let her go in peace. We had recalled our mom joking around years earlier saying, "If I ever come to a place when you would need to decide, please pull the plug." We all knew that our mom had made the decision through us. This all happened on December 24, 2014—Christmas Eve. The experience has made me a much more empathetic and compassionate person toward moms in general. Whenever I see anybody talking to their mom disrespectfully, I would say, "Be kind. Watch the way you speak to your mom!"

Your mom sounded like a lovely lady. What's the most memorable advice you've received?

The late Donald McKayle, Artistic Director of the UC Irvine dance department and my mentor, always emphasized to his students, "Finish what you start. Always finish what you start!" That advice stuck with me throughout all the productions I did. During my five years touring on the road, I always heard Mr. McKayle's advice, with his distinctive voice, like James Earl Jones, in my consciousness. After one year on tour with *The Lion King* and a total of five years on the road with three different musicals, I decided to go back to school and get my bachelor's degree—I only had one year to go. When I think about it now, the lesson I learned and the choice I made was very similar to the lesson Simba learned in *The Lion King*—"Go back and get what's rightfully yours." Two years after receiving my bachelor's degree in dance, *The Lion King* management in New York City called me out of the blue and offered me a job on Broadway.

Is there a book that has made an impact on you?

On my desk, I have this book called *The Artist's Way* by Julia Cameron. It's a helpful book in the way of guiding artists out of obstacles and roadblocks. I've read and worked through the book before, so the pages are all tattered and torn. I picked it up again because I was feeling blocked as a choreographer. Since I'm going to create a piece at my alma mater, I need to find my inspiration and purpose. I took this book out to recharge, think differently and help me find the story I want to share.

Is there a lesson that you have had to learn over and over again?

For me, it would be to "not take things personally." I learned that from the book *The Four Agreements* by Don Miguel Ruiz. Being a performing artist demands being on point and using constructive criticism to become better. There are high expectations from others and self. Not taking things personally allows me to stay focused and continue to be a professional. Is there anything that keeps you up at night? I normally sleep like a log, just ask my husband. Ha! I love to sleep.

What message would you like to give to the readers of my book who are in their 40s and beyond, who are interested in doing something different—or maybe they want to have a family, or maybe they want to try something new—what advice or thoughts do you have for them?

The time is NOW! Listen to your spirit and everything will fall into place. Create a positive and healthy internal dialogue for yourself. If we spoke to our best friend the way we sometimes speak to ourselves, I don't know if they would want to be our best friend anymore. What I'm saying is: We need to check ourselves in the way we (internally) treat ourselves. Being a yoga teacher, I observe my students' body language; when they fall out of a posture, I see how they react. I would see people getting down in the dumps and shake their heads in disappointment because they fall out of a posture. It's OK to fall! Falling is not failing—giving up is failing. I kindly remind them that it's all about getting back into their posture with determination and self-compassion.

My business partner, Karine Plantadit, mentioned that in every decade of our lives we need to revitalize ourselves; learn a different craft, travel, learn new information. We often hear people say, "Oh, I'm 60 now, I've learned it all." Well, they're just stopping themselves from learning and developing, and our brains were designed to learn. Having a business through the Kamochi Method, I have enabled myself to continue to grow and discover all the wonders of this world and my internal world—quite magical, I would say. ■

@mokshamochi @kamochimethod
@kamochiandyou @pukawinartsandwellness

SOMETIMES
ONE STEP
BACKWARDS
IS PROGRESS.

-TSHIRT SLOGAN

PEGGY WESSELINK

Could you tell me a little bit about your childhood? Did you know what you wanted to be when you grew up?

I wanted to be a cowboy or a lawyer. I had an active imagination. My older siblings—I am the youngest of four—tell stories about my imaginary friends. When I was probably 4 or 5, I had a constant companion, Donny, who one day "jumped out the window, ran across the street and was hit by a car." That was the end of my imaginary friend world. As a person, I value honesty and was taught from an early age to always tell the truth. I love to read, and I am physically active. Those are lifelong traits.

You thought you might want to be a lawyer or a cowboy. What did you end up taking in college and what did you do?

That ambition was lost around the time I hit puberty. I began struggling in school in sixth grade. Math became challenging, but I excelled at writing and words. I lost much confidence in the years leading up to high school, where I discovered that my options were few because I was a girl. I took the path I found most interesting, acceptable and likely to give me a vocation/job, nursing. Unfortunately, my instructor was extremely hard on me when I needed encouragement the most, and I dropped out to get married after the first semester. My husband was older and had just started his dream of farming. I became depressed on the farm—I didn't know how to do anything. So, I learned. I learned how to garden and that potatoes grew underground. I learned to drive a double-clutch tractor and plow the land. I learned to bake bread and produce almost all of our food. I took a correspondence course, bought 100 pregnant ewes and learned sheep farming—though not from the correspondence course! I also found a job. I was taking a tennis class, and my doubles partner said, "Go to my company and interview with the human resources person and see if maybe he can hire you for a job." The HR person asked me if I had any clerical skills, and I told him I could play the piano a little. I was hired on the spot as a secretary, and the owner's wife, who was the other secretary, fired me

after the boss asked me to go on a sales trip with him!

So, I thought, I'm going back to nursing school. I found a nearby community college, applied and finished the LPN diploma. I discovered I was pregnant with my daughter days before graduation, but I took a job in the hospital anyway. After she was born, I took various part-time nursing gigs, did some volunteer work and raised my daughter who was joined by her brother two years later.

Unfortunately, the farm went broke in the 1980s shake-up and my husband and I began looking for jobs off the land. He went back to teaching at the community college, and I applied for anything that made money. I landed a job as a stockbroker with full training included. I took it.

Wow. Then what?

I did the best I could and made money, but it was an unhappy time. I quit the job after three years, and at the age of 29, headed to the University of Iowa to get my Bachelor of Science in nursing. Although I loved the medical world, I also loved political life, and I took several classes in political science. The chair of the department saw my potential and recruited me into the doctoral program; I earned my PhD in political science.

My first teaching job was at the University of South Florida in Tampa. It was a short-term visiting assistant job, three years. I loved it! Then I moved on to earn tenure in the SUNY system of New York. Tenure was a great reward, but I was still looking for something else, but I didn't know what.

You moved from Tampa to New York and then back to Tampa? Where did the whole desire to open a restaurant and bar come from?

I'd always toyed with the idea of a small family business, and one day I just decided to make the move. I was also teaching at the college in St. Petersburg, and I figured I'd go back to it when the restaurant failed. I had a safety net, but I didn't need it. The restaurant was a financial success, and we sold it after 10 years.

Amazing. Then I heard you wanted to open a bar? How did that happen?

I realized that I could no longer work with my husband. The marriage had been in trouble for years, and I thought it might be the business, but it was us. We parted ways, and I opened a whiskey/cocktail bar. I figured I knew the business; I could see the possibilities and thought I knew how to "do" hospitality smarter. Turns out I did. I love my job. It may be the first one to really give me satisfaction and income!

Do you have any advice for anybody who might be in their midlife and is wanting to try something different and is nervous about it, or maybe they think that they can't? Any words of wisdom?

One needs to embrace the possibility of defeat and incorporate creative perseverance. There is much uncertainty in the early going, leading to tears and laughter. Know you are not alone. I turned to books, but podcasts work too. I wanted to read how other people managed their businesses and their lives! I also started small with the least capital at risk.

Midlife isn't all that much different. You think you have more to lose, but you are also more aware of what losing time, money or whatever means. And if what you gain are fun, joy and satisfaction, then it's often worth it. In midlife, you are also more aware of your one life to live, and you have more confidence in things working out. They often do.

Best or most memorable advice you've ever received?

"Embrace ambiguity and meaning." (I read that in a book by James Hollis.)

What book have you read that has made an impact on your life?

Probably two. *What Matters Most* by James Hollis and *Mountains Beyond Mountains* by Paul Farmer. I'm encouraged by people who have a passion and dedication for something and then they do it.

How about a lesson that you have had to learn over and over again?

Some people are not working toward a resolution. They're not even thinking about it. As far as coming to an agreement over something, they're happy enough to dismiss it, forget it or have it end acrimoniously. I like resolution, and I assumed others would too. I now know I may be requesting something from them that's not even possible. ■

SHANNON HUGHES

Tell me a little bit about you as a kid. What was it like for you growing up?

As an only child, I had a lot of time on my own, which I filled with make-believe and creating things. I'd hang out in the basement, building things out of Popsicle sticks, pretending to be a professional craftswoman of some sort. I'd choreograph and perform dance routines and one-act plays for my parents and their friends during dinner parties. And I spent loads of time writing short stories modeled after Stephen King in my preteen years too. I loved Stephen King! My parents were—and still are—big world travelers, so I was fortunate to be able to visit Mexico, various countries in Europe, and even when I was 12, the Amazon rain forests in Brazil. I was born and raised in the Bay Area, and I now live in the house I grew up in. It's pretty wild raising our two boys in the exact same place I spent my childhood. My older son is very sweet and sensitive and a little type A, like I was at his age. My second-grader got the stubborn independence and creative spirit.

Favorite hobbies? Did you know what you wanted to be when you grew up?

For the longest time, I wanted to be a veterinarian. It was my dream. That is until I spent a few weeks interning at an animal hospital near my home when I was about 13 and was asked to help in surgery to reattach a rabbit's eye that had been scratched violently by a house cat. That was kind of it for me.

After that, I'm pretty sure it was to be an actress or a writer—or both! I performed in community theater starting at age 7 or so and went on to write, direct and perform in high school drama. I was a theater major during my first two years of college. There's nothing like being part of a theater ensemble. I've honestly never been able to match that level of love and shared support. Hence, my love of solo shows and the eight-week classes I've been (consistently) signing up for to discover, write and prepare for them. My happy place for sure.

Can you share a little bit about your career path? What did that look like?

For my entire childhood, my dad co-owned and managed a gift show production company called Western Exhibitors. Starting in my early teens, I spent every summer in his office or on the show floor, learning about business and marketing in drips and drabs. So, after college, it made sense to pursue a career in marketing and advertising.

Six months after graduating from college, I moved to New York City and got a job with my dad's company, a bit upstate in Westchester, managing the Dallas Gift Show. When the commute and the growth opportunity ran their course, I left for a job with an internet tracking company and then onto Monster.com—then, the most prominent job search engine. Monster.com was purchased by a larger company, TMP Worldwide, and in 2002, I was transferred through TMP back home to the Bay Area.

I stayed with TMP for 16 more years, bringing my career with that company to a whopping total of 18 years! And in March 2018, I resigned from TMP and my corporate life, probably for good. Now, I'm onto big and bright adventures in entrepreneurship, bringing improv theater into business, plus starting a voice-over career. Living my dreams, truly.

I heard you might be shifting into new endeavors. Can you share more about that?

Yes, indeed. After I knew I was leaving TMP, I dove back into the creative life I'd left behind so many years ago when I decided to pursue a "real career," and that started with getting back into improv. In summer 2017, I signed up for my first class with Bay Area Theater Sports (BATS) in San Francisco, and I was totally hooked. I took one class after another and the more involved I got, the more awakened I was to just about everything else I'd been so in love with as a kid: writing, acting, voice-over study, solo show performance, deeper community involvement through The Hivery. I just kept saying, "Yes!" and everything else fell into place.

Now, almost two years after that first improv class, I'm following what I feel is my true calling: to enliven others through experiential learning, story and play. And I hope to do this through my new business—while pursuing my voice-over career and keeping up with my solo shows, which I don't think I can live without, at this point.

What's one life experience that has shaped your character?

Wow, that's a big question. I guess I'd have to say: being an only child left to my own devices to entertain myself. I'm not sure I would have become so creatively resourceful and expressive if I'd had siblings to spend all that time with. Don't get me wrong—I did have a very close friend who basically lived with us, so I wasn't totally alone. But the hours my sons spend wrestling or playing together, I spent writing, make-believing or recording pretend radio shows where I was both the DJ, the interviewer and the guests! So yeah, I suppose being an only child would answer that question.

Best or memorable advice you've received?

My parents always said: Finish what you start. It doesn't need to be perfect or prize winning, but getting it done is important.

My coach, more recently, advised me to find and live in the place between being and doing. In that place, I will find flow and truth and abundance. I go back to that again and again. It's so true. She went further to ascribe being with feminine energy and doing with masculine energy, which I'd also never heard before—but find fascinating and come back to that frequently as well.

Best book you've read or one that has made a great impact?

As a kid: *The Giving Tree*—you just can't beat the message in that book. Timeless and so powerful!

As an early teen: Anything written by Stephen King. I idolized the man and just recently loved his book, *On Writing*, which made me fall for him all over again!

More recently: *Big Magic* by Elizabeth Gilbert, anything written by Mark Nepo and, of course, *The Artist's Way* by Julia Cameron, which I'm pretty sure changed my life two years ago when I woke up to my creativity again.

What's the lesson you've had to learn over and over?

I am enough. What I perceive as other people's impressions of me doesn't matter. Keep coming back to who I am and why I'm loved.

Perfection doesn't exist. My search for perfection has often stood in the way of being true to my voice/message, especially in my writing and performance. Authenticity always rules over perfection.

White wine makes me feel yucky the day after. That's one I'm not sure I'll ever truly learn.

What, if anything, keeps you up at night?

These past few years, it's exciting energy: What will I create next? What should the focus of my show be? Am I ready for my first workshop at The Hivery? Did I sign up for the workshop that was just announced? And, of course, because I'm a human being and a mom/wife/daughter—all the other domestic brain noise around to-do lists and deadlines. And I know I'm not alone on that one!

What message would you like to impart to our readers who are on the fence about jumping into something new?

We are all born creators. Making things is in our blood, brought to us through hundreds of years of ancestors telling stories, building, weaving, painting, cooking, writing, creating. And most often not for money—but just for the love and tradition of it. For community and heart centeredness. To feel whole and part of something bigger at the same time.

Don't wait for soon, or later, or even next year. Those are not dates on the calendar, they are just warnings from your fear, whose job it is to keep you from showing up in this world. Just dive into what you love and start anywhere. ∎

/shannondeanhughes   @shannondeanhughes   blog: www.living-unscripted.com   www.shannondeanhughes.com

let the beauty
we love be
what we do.
there are hundreds
of ways to kneel
& kiss the
ground.

♡

-RUMI

TEAL SKY HELLER

Would you mind sharing a little bit about what it was like for you as a kid? Did you know what you wanted to be when you grew up?

I was born and raised here in Alaska. My mom was also born and raised here, and my dad came to Alaska in the first grade. I was one of the only kids in school with both sets of grandparents in town. That was kind of interesting because I had a huge family in a community that did not have extended families. Alaska is where people go to run away, so most people rarely have family here. So, I grew up with this massive extended family, loving life.

We lived on the side of a mountain. My grandpa had homesteaded a hundred acres in the Eagle River Valley. The nearest neighbor was a mile away. I would read about things like sidewalks and city blocks. I didn't know how long a block was. I have two older sisters, I'm the youngest. We grew up with just the mountain as our playground. We'd get followed home by bears, run into a moose. Our pets would get eaten by bears, and that was just kind of life. We had lots of animals—goats and chickens and everything. Our family commercially fished for red salmon in Bristol Bay from grade school through college. My sisters and I were my dad's crew, and we had countless adventures on the high seas. When I was 12, our house burned down, so we moved to town. My dad kind of quit functioning at that point. From the age of 12 to when I moved away from home at 18, it was a very rough home life. He wasn't functioning, and he ended up spending time in a halfway house. I went from this very idyllic lifestyle with a very tight-knit family to the point where we were waiting for the cops to show up. My parents divorced, and I was the kid that was like, "Finally."

Two of us sisters coped by becoming very successful in school, going to college with lots of academic scholarships. Throughout college, I worked three jobs in addition to school. I had no school debt when I finished. I graduated from college with a degree in theater and history, and I went off to Fairbanks, Alaska, to do youth work with Young Life. So that's kind of how I grew up.

Oh, wow. So, you went to college, and you were in theater. How would you say your career path evolved?

I was an early youth worker, and I didn't date very much, so I ended up marrying my first boyfriend. I was 24, 25, somewhere around there, and did not have experience in relationships at all. That turned out badly. I ended up staying home with my two kids for eight years, so I went from being a youth worker to making zero money. I volunteered at the high school because I worked with high school kids to design costumes. I also had the occasional stagehand job for shows that came to town. Well, as many as I could, but there was my family to consider. When my kids were super little, I was designing costumes in Anchorage, because I could bring them with me to the costume shop. My son, I could throw him in a backpack and go work in the costume shop, and it was great. But my daughter was the polar opposite, very active and a huge handful. Which is hilarious, because nowadays, she's not the handful—he is.

I was staying home with my kids, doing theater on the side. Then, I started my own business. I designed and sold my hand-spun yarns and taught knitting and quilting classes. When my youngest headed out to school, I knew I needed to get a job. My husband was not steadily providing for us any longer. As I looked for a job, I came across a pamphlet about the top 20 fastest-growing jobs in Alaska. One of them was computer-aided drafting.

I had done a little bit of that with theater set design. I thought I'd try it. I took one class and said, "Yeah, I could do this." I needed to find a way to pay for school because we had no money. We would make the mortgage payment each month and that was about it. At the same time, we built our own house while living in a tent, until it got too cold. Two toddlers in a tent on a building site. It was a little intense. Around then, my daughter was diagnosed with juvenile rheumatoid arthritis. She would cry every night, and she hurt all the time. So, we started this journey of giving her massive drugs. You just cringe at the idea of giving drugs to little kids, but this arthritis could destroy my child. We

needed to be able to afford the doctors and medical care, so I applied for a grant to fund my education. The American Association of University Women has a career development grant, a worldwide competitive scholarship. And I got it!

Congrats! What happened next?

The grant was for women re-entering the workforce who already have a degree. I wrote an essay about my daughter, dealing with her arthritis as my inspiration, so that I could also face this big change of going back into the workforce. The $11,000 grant funded my first year of school. It helped pay for childcare, parking, a new computer and all my class materials.

So that was how I got started. While taking my second drafting class, I heard about an electrical engineering company that was hiring part time. I didn't have prior classes in that field. By then, I was desperate. I had worked off and on, teaching lessons on how to quilt and knit but had nothing like a career.

I called this company for a part-time job, as I figured the worst they could do is say no. I was 35. At the interview, they asked, "Do you have experience?" I reply, "No, I'm a student at UAA," trying to avoid telling them I'm only in my second drafting class.

They hired me that day. I would go to classes at UAA in the morning and work for the company in the afternoon. At the end of the workday, my boss would tell me what I'd be doing the next day. I'd tell my professor in the morning, "This is what I'm going to be doing at work. How do I do it?" I started on a big civil project, and I happened to be in civil drafting at the time. My professor would teach me what I needed to do that day at work and then I would go to work and do it. So, I learned in the morning how to do what I needed to do in the afternoon. I kept my mouth shut, showed up on time and paid attention. And what I learned is that if you show up sober and wanting to learn, employers will keep you. That was nine years ago. I always told people I accidentally got into electrical engineering. I worked for the same company for the next 10 years, although I moved up within the company. I ended my time there as an elec-

trical designer, bidding and running my own jobs. They contracted me out to local utilities. I designed commercial lighting, industrial lighting, electrical utilities in subdivisions and streetlights.

With a degree in theater. So, you went back to school for engineering. Did you finish your degree?

No, I didn't finish the degree program. The University of Alaska Anchorage has an associate degree program called the Architectural and Engineering Technology program. And I figured I might as well I get a job in engineering technology because it was listed as one of the top 20 jobs in Alaska. There's a poor graduation rate because everyone gets a job in the program and leaves school before graduation.

So, I got a job and left the program. I did receive another scholarship to continue in the program for the second year. But by then I would ask questions like, "This is what I do at work. Will your electrical drafting class teach me how to do this, that, etc.?" They'd say, "No, you won't learn that." So, I dropped out when my company offered me a full-time position.

I had a good-paying job, so from then on, I learned on the job. I'm not an engineer; I'm an electrical designer. I create all the designs and then an engineer signs off on my work.

It's a very technical job that I didn't plan on doing as a career. I woke up eight years later and wondered, "What am I doing? How did I get here?" And then I started asking myself, "Where do I go next?" It was sort of a personality test. I'm pretty much working 100% in my weakest areas, which makes me very good at what I do because I'm overcompensating. I'm so bad at the things I need to do for my job that I super overcompensate with the details and organization.

What is next for you?

I started looking around trying to figure out what I really want to do. I had owned a lot of small businesses that never made money—never. I owned an art gallery before I had children. The art gallery was called The Finer Things. I sold fine and functional art—my own art as well as others'. I've always been pulled toward making functional artwork. I remarried a few years ago, and my husband can build anything. I said to him, "I have ideas for these lights. Can you teach me how to build them?" He said, "sure." So, I started making light fixtures. I made all the fixtures for the home we live in now. The light fixtures in the common areas are made out of pipe and sound projects. The sconces are made of transmission parts, camping cups and a lot of different things. I worked on a business plan of selling these lights. I kept the name Snarl Design that I'd used way back with my fiber business because that's kind of how my brain works; it's just a snarl of creative ideas. The lights sold incredibly well.

However, I found that I'm creative and can design lots of things, but I'm not so great at the physical construction, like crimping the wires and seeing how two parts can go together. I can see what I want to do mentally, but I could not get the two parts together.

One day, I was working on some tall floor lamps. They were super heavy pipe lamps, about 6, 7 feet tall. I had prewired everything. My husband picked it up to do finish work on it, and the wires literally fell out of the lamp. He said, "You know, you're going to kill someone."

I knew it wasn't my husband's dream to build my lights. And I do not have the technical skills to be building these lights. So, I put Snarl Design on hold for the sake of the marriage.

I might come back to lighting one day. I might find an electrician who wants to work with me making those great lights. But for now, the idea is shelved. And I kept looking for what it was that I wanted to do. About this time, I started listening to the Cathy Heller podcast, *Don't Keep Your Day Job*.

What was next on your horizon?

I can't eat gluten, but I love to bake, so I put together a business plan for a gluten-free bakery. I crunched the numbers and joined a business class online that I'm still a part of.

I did all of the pre-business work, priced up the recipes, tested recipes, wrote out my daily schedule and all that. When I finished, I was like, "Oh, my gosh,

this is a bakery." I never wanted to have a storefront. I wanted to sell to coffee shops and restaurants. I realized I would need make deliveries at 6:00 a.m. We'd have to start baking around 10:00 p.m. or midnight. That's not the lifestyle I wanted.

Also, we like to get out in the woods. We do a lot of rafting, hiking, camping, all that. We don't want to be tied down on the weekends. We want to be outdoors. So, it was on to the next plan.

Since I deal with utilities—the first step of subdivisions and dealing with what's in the ground—I was like, "Maybe I should be a real estate agent." My husband said, "That's awesome. That's perfect for you. You like people. You can use your brain." I really did well in school, and I learned engineering on the fly, so I figured I could learn real estate.

Real estate is not as painstaking as engineering and works more in my areas of strength. So, I decided I'd give it a try. All the while I had to keep in mind that I'm not failing at all the other things. Life is written in pencil. That became my mantra.

The hard thing was everyone kept asking about the light fixture business because they had sold really well. But I don't need to burn down anyone's house. So, I started studying for my real estate test, signed up for a class and started researching how to do it well.

In the middle of all this, my dad died in the summer. He wasn't that great of a father. What really hit me, and I totally didn't expect it, was that I had to grieve the lost hope that he would become a good dad. The good thing is that my husband and I had spent some time visiting him in Oregon before he passed away, and our relationship was in the best place that it had been in decades. We never stopped speaking or anything like that. It's just, you don't get to pick your relatives, so they're not always your best friend.

We were in a really good place, and I had no regrets when he died. There wasn't anything unfinished. But it was hard to give up that dream that one day he'd become a good dad. So, that kind of slowed my real estate studies. I became licensed in August 2018. I was still working full time with the engineering firm but looking at a plan of getting into real estate full time within two to three years. I started branding my real estate foray as an adventure, like buying into the adventure of living in Alaska. That's where I want to go with it. I used to have all sorts of interests, and life just keeps knocking you down, and what I want in my life is that sense of adventure.

And would you say that was a life experience that has shaped your character?

Commercial fishing was a huge character shaper for me and not necessarily in a good way. There's just this essence of never giving up and keep going no matter what. The fish keep coming, so you have to clean the net. You can't say, "I'm tired." You just keep working. And I think that's probably contributed a lot to my basic work ethic of never quitting.

My adrenal glands don't work either, so I've been tired for—I don't know—going on 20 years. I'm pretty much old. I think part of what commercial fishing taught me is how to be tough, which is often great, and I'm proud of it. It's something I would never trade. But it's also taught me never to quit, and sometimes it's healthy to quit.

I think that that was also what my engineering job gave me, because as a single mom, I was able to keep that job and not have to worry about money as long as I showed up to work. But it wore me out, never quitting.

In conclusion: I surpassed my goals, and I left engineering school after only one year! I am doing real estate full time. I love it. I feel like I have finally found a way to live in my strengths and serve others.

What is the best or most memorable advice that you've received? Something that you take forward with you?

Life is written in pencil. Like what am I living with now—that's life written in pencil. And not to have any regrets for what I've done. One day at a time.

Is there a book you have read that has made an impact on you, or one you would recommend?

One of the things with being exhausted is that at work I use my eyes and my brain constantly. I used to read massively. I read tons of books as part of my book club that we started back in college and still meet monthly. But I don't read anymore because my brain is tired, which is why I'm addicted to podcasts. One that has really made an impact on me is Cathy Heller's *Don't Keep Your Day Job.*

How about a lesson you've had to learn over and over again?

How to rest—I do not know how to do it.

What message would you like to leave our readers?

One step at a time. I think most people our age are working full-time jobs. They're not going to be able to drop everything and find a new path. So, that means we all have to take little steps every single day. "What am I going to do today toward finding my dream?"

So, I love painting. I have no particular skill with it, but I love painting. What I found is that I have all sorts of excuses to not paint. And the reality is I just need to go do it. That's probably why I'm not pursuing art as a business. I think that asking ourselves, "What am I doing today?" can take us to the next place. ∎

 @tealsky907

Could you tell me a little bit about what growing up was like for you? Do you have any favorite hobbies and did you know what you wanted to be when you grow up?

I grew up the eldest of five children in a working-class family in Ireland. As a kid I was not quiet, but I was definitely reserved. I was attentive, studious, an overachiever who skipped two grades in secondary school and graduated at 16. As a kid, I was very independent. I had big dreams for myself, even though at the time, those dreams weren't clear to me. I just knew I wanted more out of life than what I saw ahead for myself. At the time, the economy was very, very poor. The unemployment rate was extremely high. I did not like the future I saw for myself. I had this pride and ambition to do something. At the time, I just didn't know what that was.

WE'RE ALL IN THE GUTTER BUT SOME OF US ARE LOOKING AT THE STARS.

- OSCAR WILDE

Throughout secondary school, I knew I wanted to be a teacher. I grew up in a country, and at a time, when there was no expectation of going to college. My peers were not going to college either. There was no money for higher education, and it's not something that was talked about at home.

Did you have any hobbies when you were little, or were you focused on school?

A lot of the hobbies were related to school in some way or another: mostly extracurricular activities and sports, like tennis. I followed an amateur boxing club as a teenager. Spending time with parents, family, friends. I have over 100 cousins. We all grew up together and spent a lot of time together. The family unit kept us occupied.

And so, you graduated from high school at 16 and then what did you do?

I did nothing for a couple of years. I went to work in a factory. The factory made and assembled computer parts. It was the most monotonous job, but at least I had a job. I had only been at it three weeks when on Christmas Eve, the boss came to us and said, "OK, we lost our contract, everybody is done." I thought, "Oh, this is definitely not the life I want for myself." I started thinking, what can I do? I decided before I step into this life that I know is ahead of me, I want to be able to do something for myself, so I can look back and go, "OK, well, at least I did something for myself."

I was thinking about going to Canada, although I wasn't quite sure what I was going to do, but we had family there. I was looking at that, and then someone said, "Hey, why don't you go to Washington, D.C., and be a nanny?" And I said, "Well, OK." And keep in mind that Ireland is a tiny island nation. I had no idea what I was agreeing to. I had no understanding of the scope or the size of this country or the cultures, and the diversity. I had nothing, but it seemed like the way out of where I was. I agreed to go. I came over to the United States at the age of 19, on a one-way ticket with $150 in my pocket, to a country where I didn't know anyone—but I had a nanny job lined up.

And were your parents and family supportive?

They were supportive, but they would have preferred that I didn't leave. They also knew why I was doing it and saw for themselves that there were limited opportunities for me in Ireland.

You were the first of your family to leave?

Yes. And we were a close extended family. It was hard for them to see me leave. And so, I took the nanny job for 12 months, which turned into seven years, and here I am 34 years later.

What an amazing story. Do you mind sharing a little bit of your progression to where you are now?

I worked as a nanny. I lived in for four years and then lived out for three years, but I was with that same family for seven years. I was very blessed. I found a great family, and as the kids got older and they went to school, I started school, and I was there for them when they came home. Eventually, I began the teaching career I had dreamed of. For many years, I taught special education to middle and high school kids with severe emotional and behavioral disorders.

I did that for 10 years. While I was doing that, I bartended around Washington, D.C. That evolved into event planning. I always had a second job while I was a teacher, all while finishing up my teaching credential. I was starting to burn out from teaching special education, when someone offered me a job working as an events contractor, and my salary doubled overnight. I did that for a couple of years and then I landed a job for a global hotel company at their corporate headquarters doing international human resources.

So, you got into HR?

I worked for this hotel company in human resources for eight years. I loved everything about them as a company, but I was miserable in my job. I found myself working in an environment that was very unhealthy. I couldn't figure out how to get out but still stay with the company. I tried to make lateral moves within the company, but the management of my department just wouldn't support my move. So, I figured out how to make my move.

*While you were working doing your day job,
how are you building your side business, Capital
Coat Check?*

While I was working, I had some life events where I could have used the support of my supervisors, and I didn't get it. I started looking outside of the company. I knew I wanted to go into events planning. I had started talking to some of the hotels, but in the hotel environment, the pay is very, very low, and the hours are awful.

During this time, my daughter was sick, and I took leave to take care of her. While I was on leave, I decided not to return to my job. It was one of the easiest decisions I've ever made. I knew I wanted to be an event planner, and I knew I wanted to work for myself. I also knew that this wasn't going to happen unless I made it happen. The timing felt right. So I did it.

Good for you. That is bravery. Then what?

On August 6, 2013, I registered the business with the State of Maryland. That's how I got to have an event planning business. I enjoyed teaching, and I always wanted to work for myself. I kind of had that little entrepreneurial bug. I had to figure out how to blend these things.

I began by taking on small events, small weddings. I worked my way into high-end weddings, and while I was doing that, a hotel called me and said, "Sorry for the short notice, could you come in on the 7th of January to do coat check? We have an event—we need a coat check."

I had no idea how to do a coat check service. I had no equipment. I had nothing. And I'm thinking, "Oh my goodness." And I said, "Sure, no problem."

And then, they said, "Well, in that case, can you do an event New Year's Eve?" This was on the 29th of December! I said, "Sure." I ran out and hired 16 people; I got uniforms, did a little bit of research and hoped I was pricing it accordingly. And, of course, when I gave my price they kept going, "Are you sure? Well, what about this and what about that?" And I'm like, "Well, clearly, I'm not pricing this right, but…"

So, my first coat checking was New Year's Eve at one of the largest hotels in the country! We pulled it off. Other hotels started booking us and then it started to become a little overwhelming. I was having an identity crisis. Am I an event planner or am I checking coats? I could see the potential for the money and the business, so I started the second company called Capital Coat Check. I began to market that, and I've been doing that now for a few years. That is truly where my time and devotion goes. I still have the event planning business, and I still do some of that in the off-season, but I put my heart and soul into the coat check, which seems like the most bizarre business.

But there's a need, and you're filling that need.

Yes, there is. We are the only true coat and bag check operations company in the D.C. markets for hundreds of miles in any direction. And we are digital. So, I have the exclusive rights to a digital system that I bought from the designers of the software. And so, while everybody else issues a paper ticket, and the papers get lost and tickets fall off the hangers, we have a digital system and none of that happens. We have set ourselves apart by being the only true coat and bag check operations company in our market, and we can do very high-volume events. We just did one for 10,000 people on New Year's Eve, just one event.

When I went out to your website, I thought, I've never heard of this type of service outside of a hotel or restaurant.

What's interesting is at first, I had no website. So many people were asking, "Where is your website? I can't find you." So, I ran out in a hurry and got a website, and all of a sudden people were able to find me. Everybody is finding me. Now when anyone Googles "D.C. Coat Check," I come up. I'm getting all these inbound inquiries.

This is very niche and so interesting how you got to where you are. Thank you for sharing. My next question is: What is the life experience that has shaped your character?

The death of my brother and the death of my mother. I look at life very differently now. Also, being a single parent has helped shape me into who I am. Every time there's a new event, it's my focus and my priority. I don't get upset about the little things in life. I do not judge people. I was never one for judging people, but I do not judge people, because you just don't know what they're dealing with. Life keeps throwing things at you. You are constantly adapting and changing,

What is the best or most memorable piece of advice that you have received?

You will not get what you deserve; you will get what you negotiate.

Best book you've read or one that made an impact on you?

Eat That Frog by Brian Tracy. I take what I have learned from that little book and practice it every day. I taught it to my sister and my daughter. We use that all the time. If I'm complaining about something or struggling, my sister will say right back at me, "You know what, you just need to eat that frog."

A lesson you have had to learn over and over?

I'm more resilient than I think I am. Another lesson I have learned is that when I hear "no," it doesn't always mean no. Sometimes it means not now.

What message would you like to leave for our readers who are on the fence about trying something they're passionate about?

I would say follow your heart, trust yourself and just go for it. ∎

@capitalcoatcheck   www.capitalcoatcheck.com

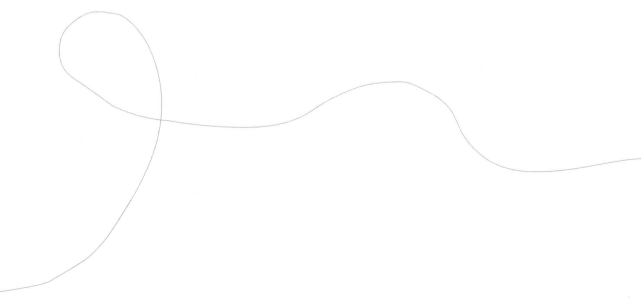

VICTORIA DAVIS

Tell me a little bit about your childhood. What was it like for you growing up? Did you know what you wanted to be when you grew up?

I didn't know what to call what I wanted to be when I grew up, but eventually, I learned it was industrial/organizational (I/O) psychology! That's what was going to solve my family's challenges. Growing up, it was my younger brother, me, my mom and dad. Dad came from a small family. Mom had three sisters, and they each had between two and six children. Work was a big part of our family life. We worked to live.

Mom was at home with us in the early years: working part-time hourly jobs and selling Avon, that sort of thing. My dad was a charter bus driver: driving tour groups from New York all across the United States, plus sometimes Canada and Mexico. For a number of years, he tended to be away more than he was home. When I was 11, my dad got laid off. Though both were applying for work, my mom was the first one who got a full-time job, so my dad became a bit of a Mr. Mom until he also got a full-time job a few months later. At that point, my brother and I became latchkey kids. Mom worked late afternoons into the overnight shift while dad worked during the day. Mom got us off to school in the mornings, my brother and I would come home in the afternoons and get ourselves settled, then Dad would take care of us in the evenings.

As a teen, I guess I started to think about jobs and careers. My thinking back then was that "jobs really screwed up families." Jobs messed up my family life. Dad was now having to do things he didn't have to do before, like laundry, homework and cooking. And we barely had any family time when we were all together.

While he was in junior high school, my parents identified that my brother had a slight learning disability. My parents fought hard to get support for him from the school district while both of them worked full time. Around the same time, I started having health issues and physical challenges. I was eventually diagnosed with junior rheumatoid arthritis. So, lots of juggling was going on within our family during my teenage years.

One summer during high school, I took an introduction to psychology class at a local community college. We got to a chapter on I/O psychology and something clicked. This is a career that could help my family and others. It could be a way to fix some of the conflicts between work and family life by having an impact on the types of jobs people hold and the way work is done within organizations.

Years later, both of my parents retired from the same companies where they had started working when I was 12. Dad retired from the same company doing the same type of work he did when he started there: driving buses and some mechanic work. Mom moved all around customer service type jobs within the local cable company. She moved up a couple of levels (supervisor and manager) and worked in various departments within the organization. Thinking back, it was an interesting dynamic to see evolve.

Did you go to college? What was that path like?

In high school, before I learned about I/O psychology, I was interested in counseling or other types of support services. After volunteering for over a year at a crisis hotline, I came to feel like that type of work was too heavy for me. I became more interested in the area of work-life integration. That type of career path had more power behind it to me; it would give me an opportunity to affect more people over time. I would be able to help people and organizations by developing systems and processes that could improve work-life balance and the work environment as a whole.

In college, I initially worked on the recruiting/selection side of things to help people find their place in the world of work while not pulling their hair out. That's how I describe my time working in career services. I went to Cedar Crest College, a women's liberal arts school in Allentown, Pennsylvania. I started out studying two majors: psychology and business. Before that, I hadn't been very popular, nor did I feel super smart. I worked hard but hadn't yet found my leadership space. College changed that. I loved the environment. It was a good time for me to figure out

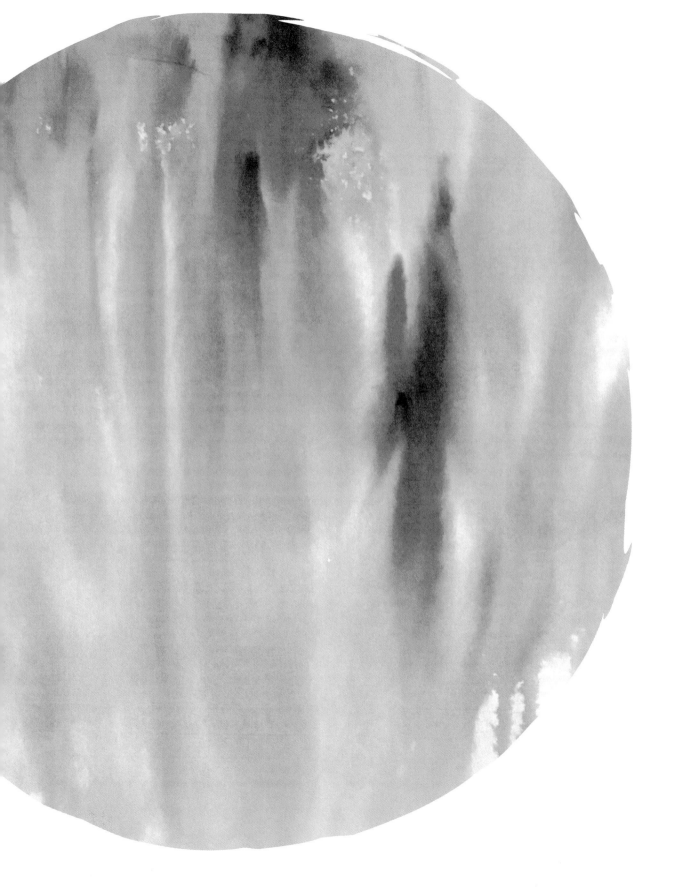

who I wanted to be. Plus, I loved that I could show up to an 8 a.m. class in my pajamas!

On the flip side, depression and anxiety reared their heads. As I mentioned, when I was 12, I was diagnosed with junior rheumatoid arthritis, so it made school extra challenging. During college, the stress of a double major, trying to finish school on time, and working to cover the cost of school was too much to juggle at once. I worked at career services, babysat for professors' children, and was part of the residence hall staff. It was a lot! In my senior year, I had to take a break. I had recently lost my grandma after my grandpa had passed away the prior year. I took the fall semester off, came home to New York, and went to therapy. In order to finish college on schedule, I ended up dropping my business major and finished with a B.A. in psychology.

During my sophomore and junior years in college, I had a cool internship through the International Foundation of Employee Benefit Plans, which helped match qualified students with human resources jobs at organizations. I worked with the NYC Office of Labor Relations. I worked there during summers and school breaks for two years while I was in college. They offered me a full-time role after graduation, and I worked there for several years after college. The first year, I just worked. My first summer after I started working, I took off a few weeks to backpack through Europe with a friend. Both the arthritis and the depression were under control, and we had a wonderful adventure!

When I got back from Europe, I continued working full time with the City of New York and started a master's degree in industrial/organizational psychology at City University of NY (CUNY) Baruch College part time at night. I got close to finishing my degree but struggled with getting thesis research off the ground. I had a temporary setback when my first thesis plan fell through. Shortly after that, I stopped working with the City of NY and took a job with a company called Interactive, Inc. Working there gave me additional ideas for my thesis, and it was a great job. I was able to continue with my professor as my thesis advisor

remotely. I had a good relationship with him and got lots of support. The business I worked at was run by a married couple. It was a research company. I did program evaluation while partnering with nonprofits and educational companies. For example, I analyzed STEM (science, technology, engineering, math) summer programs.

What impact did the programs have? How effective were they?

I used the Kirkpatrick evaluation method. These programs were funded by grants, so documenting how they worked was important. I stayed there for two years. After that, I switched coasts. I had family in San Francisco, but I was the first one to move to Southern California. I relocated to pursue my doctorate in industrial/organizational psychology at the California School of Professional Psychology (CSPP) in San Diego.

When I started school, I found my New York clique: I became friends with a woman who moved from Brooklyn and one who moved from New Jersey. I loved that the doctorate program was an applied program. A big pull for me was all the work psychologist Rodney Lowman was doing, but he moved to the LA campus right before I arrived in San Diego. I got involved in activities across campuses. I worked with career services leadership development and facilitated organizational development efforts with student life staff. I also worked at temp jobs off-campus. The year before graduation, while I was working on my dissertation, I ended up moving back to New York, where I also worked part time for the research company I was with before I had moved to San Diego.

What did you do next?

After graduation, I moved to Atlanta and took a position as an internal consultant with The Home Depot. I mostly worked in selection and executive development (assessment and development). I worked in the assessment/selection center for various layers of management jobs. I did 360 assessments and facilitated feedback sessions, full-day assessments and employee retention work. As the year was finishing up, between the heat and the bugs, I knew I wasn't going to stay in Atlanta. While I was getting interviews and flying around the country, I learned which places I really didn't want to live.

I moved back to New York for a little bit while I figured out what to do next. I took on some consulting projects and worked at temp jobs. Eventually, I landed at Marriott International in the Washington, D.C., area doing selection work. The work matched with my dissertation research, which was on how well people fit with their job, team and organization. This was in June 2008. I was there for the next six years, and during that time, I was promoted twice. I made a great group of friends. I got healthier, took up Pilates, and once again, my rheumatoid arthritis was under control. Those years, I focused on my health and that improved both my professional development and confidence. I got promoted to director of selection. I also started dating someone, but it was a long-distance relationship, as he lived in New York.

Then, I got a new leader at work. We didn't mesh well. When I learned that I wasn't her choice as part of the team's succession plan, I knew that I needed to make a change. What should I do: relocate? Stay? Look for a new job? Around the same time, the company sponsored me to take part in SHAMBAUGH's Women in Leadership and Learning Program (WILL), a coaching program facilitated by founder Rebecca Shambaugh. The coaching program reinforced for me that this professional situation wasn't working for me, and it was time to move on from the company and move toward my relationship. I started looking for a new job, one that would take me up to New York to be with my boyfriend and closer to my immediate family.

Though JPMorgan & Chase has a reputation for flexibility, my immediate supervisor didn't subscribe to it. I ended up running to different places around the city for in-person meetings; hosting overnight calls with Asia while being expected to show up at work in the city by 8 a.m.; and traveling to additional sites along the East Coast. It was physically taxing running around all day and keeping extremely long hours. My rheumatoid arthritis started flaring up and became untenable. This flipped me on my head. I've now been disabled since 2015.

I heard you might be making another life change? Could you share what's next for you?

Yes. The last several years have been overly challenging in terms of dealing with workplace stress and seeing if enough work accommodations could be made for my health issues. Unfortunately, I remain disabled and unable to work. In addition to the chronic pain from rheumatoid arthritis, I have been diagnosed with fibromyalgia, and the anxiety and depression have intensified. I am under the care of several medical professionals and continue to work with therapists toward recovery. Obtaining health insurance and disability benefits were a whole other undertaking. It's time for a refresh. My partner and I are moving to the Charlotte, North Carolina, area. We want to start a new chapter. He was presented with a job opportunity, and the location is appealing to us for a bunch of reasons, so we are relocating. We're hopeful that the change in climate and additional access to quality health care will support my recovery and open new doors.

What's a life experience that has shaped your character?

Being diagnosed with a chronic illness so early in life, I thought that I would be more resilient by now. I continue to learn lessons about persevering and being more patient, both with myself and others. I've truly been blessed to have my family and loved ones always by my side. They give me tremendous strength.

What is the best or most memorable advice you've received?

Serenity prayer! In the darkest times, that's what I think about.

Best book you've read? (or one that you just really love)

I can't think of a specific book, but I do have a favorite story from a movie. It's a film called *Grace of my Heart*, written and directed by Allison Anders. It's a great story of perseverance through hardships, of figuring out who you are and becoming a better version of yourself.

What's a lesson you've had to learn over and over?

   I am currently trying to figure out—how much do I bend without losing myself in the process?

What message would you like to impart to our readers who might be on the fence about trying something new or going for something they are passionate about?

   Something I heard from a past boss: You want people to leave you feeling better than when they came to you. If we can just do that in our daily life, we make a difference. Wouldn't that be nicer for the world? ■

MY STORY: CLARISSA CASTILLO-RAMSEY

The Younger Years…

From age 5 onward, I knew I wanted to be an artist. Drawing and painting were the things I could do all day. My parents indulged me with a painting easel, a painter's smock—even a matching beret. I remember drawing nearly every day and being so proud to show visitors my work. I liked drawing animals, specifically horses. One day, my mom and I were talking, and she asked me what I wanted to be when I grew up.

I told her I wanted to be an artist. She laughed like she thought that was funny. She told me artists only get rich and famous after they die! And, just like that, "pop!" went my dream balloon. From that moment on, I looked at art as something fun to do, but I didn't dare treat it as a serious life path. It wasn't the "right" thing to focus on. That started a limiting belief that I needed to fit into some kind of appropriate mold when it came to a career.

School Years

It was tough for me to get good grades in middle and high school. I am more of a right-brained person—a creative, abstract thinker—than someone who solves problems through logic. For most of my life, I felt out of place in a left-brained world. I had to study hard to get A's and B's. The subjects I enjoyed were art and French! How could I use those skills?

College offered new opportunities, but I felt obligated to study business. That seemed to be the "proper" thing to do. Both of my parents are physicians, and I'm grateful they did not push me and my brother and sister to medicine. At the same time, they were such high achievers that I didn't want to let them down. Surely, I couldn't do anything in the creative realm that would be too weird and unstable. I decided to get a B.S. in marketing and human resources, as those were the only two areas of business that didn't make me gag. I thought Marketing was kind of like art, right? Maybe I could find a creative pathway through a marketing degree. I thought I could be the person in advertising who comes up with creative copy or design. I also liked helping and connecting with people. I was the friend people would call when they were in a pickle or needed advice or consoling. Maybe I could find something interesting to do for the rest of my life if I went down that road. In my mind, human resources was the people side of the business, and I thought I could make an impact working in that field, helping employees navigate through difficult times at work, like I helped my friends.

While I was in the program, there was one class that I enjoyed: organizational behavior. It was a newer field in HR at that time and seemed a little "new age" and "woo." I remember thinking, there are probably no jobs in that area, I'm not going to bother. Here was another time I didn't listen to my inner voice, which was telling me to dive deeper. There was another thing some of my classmates were doing that piqued my interest. It was graphic design. By the time I learned about it, I was practically done with my undergrad, and I didn't want to take any additional classes. I just wanted to graduate!

Be the change
You wish to see
in the world

- ATTRIBUTED
To GHANDI

Working Years…

Post-graduation, my first gig was in retail management. It was a toss-up between that and working in a management training program for a car rental company. I soon discovered I disliked retail. It was tough on my feet, long hours with little pay. I found out that other people who were in the same management program were making more money than I was. I did walk away with some cool clothes, though.

Toward the end of my retail career, I started drawing, doodling again. I took a 2D design class at UMass. My memories of that class were so negative. Everyone had to post their work for crit (criticism time). I remember getting so much negative feedback on many assignments, I am surprised I finished the class. I ended up getting a B-. My teacher's parting words to me, "Just because you like a certain dance doesn't mean you can dance." I took it as, give it up, kid, you don't have a talent for the art world. Ouch! I felt defeated in that moment, but it still didn't deter me.

I decided to get out of retail. I up and moved to California to pursue my interest in graphic design. I thought it was time to go for that artistic career I had been afraid to pursue during my undergrad.

I ended up taking a few classes at The ArtCenter, College of Design in Pasadena. A new world opened for me. I met so many cool art people. During the day, I took any old temp job to pay the bills. Eventually, I found an institution where I could get a graphic design certificate: Platt College in Eagle Rock, California. I enrolled in the fall of 1997, and that started a new career chapter. It was a tough schedule. I worked a 9-to-5 job. Then, I had class from 6 p.m. to 10 p.m., Monday through Friday—but if you want something bad enough, you do it, right? I met more great people, some of whom I am still friends with today. A word to the wise: Make connections wherever you are. Collaboration over competition with your colleagues.

Post-program, finding work in graphic design was difficult. I applied to different places and got rejected over and over again. I had to keep temping to pay the bills and took on jobs I didn't like or want to stay in. My mom sent tons of encouragement cards and reminded me that I would succeed and not to give up. Eventually, one of my classmates helped me get connected with a creative agency. The account executive advised me to continue to hone my graphic skills as mine were, frankly, just average. After a year or so of going to the agency and practicing my Illustrator, Photoshop, and QuarkXPress skills, I got some footing in the graphic design world. At first, the jobs were very short-term, a few days, a week. I had to supplement my time with the other staffing agencies I'd signed up for so I could continue working and pay my bills. Eventually, the creative work became steady. I temped at different organizations and started going back to companies that knew me. It was kind of nice being a free agent.

In 2000, one of the temp agencies I worked with—Hart Employment Services—told me about a job they thought would be up my alley. It was not their typical administrative work, but they knew I went to design school. The company was The Coffee Bean & Tea Leaf, and the position was for a production artist. This is where I learned so much about the corporate world: working with people and leading people. I spent almost seven years there and was promoted to graphic designer and left as the graphic design manager. I satisfied the interest I had in college to explore this career. Toward the end of my time at The Bean, I started painting again. I missed the fun times I had as a child, creating to create and self-express. In graphic design, you're doing what your client wants; not necessarily what you want to design. If you're a fine artist, you're creating what you want to create.

In the early to mid-2000s, I started going to church with one of my graphic design friends. We would go to Sunday or Wednesday service at Agape International Spiritual Center. The church was filled with these mystical paintings by an artist called Rassouli. We met him and started taking his classes at Agape. We started to go to his art retreats, where we met up with other amazing artists. For me, it was another time for "rebirth." These people were my tribe! I hadn't been around a group of artists in a long time, and I felt seen and understood with this group. It was such a contrast with the corporate world. I felt like I could let my hair down and just be. In the evenings at these retreats, we would sit in a circle and go around the room and just talk about how we felt, what insights we had about our creations, what we learned that day. Rassouli taught about painting with heart, letting things flow, embracing your creative self. One of my favorite things he asked us to do during the retreats was to switch canvases mid-painting with our neighbor. It was an exercise in detachment. That practice taught me the value of letting go.

Back at work, I was getting antsy, asking myself things like, "Is this it?" "What do I want next?" "Do I still want to pursue this graphic design thing?" I felt like I had reached a good point in my creative career. I believe there was something about painting again—and the lessons contained therein—that helped me realize this. I knew I didn't want my boss' job. I didn't have any desire to become the art director anywhere… so what's next?

During my time at The Coffee Bean, I had made my interest in HR known and had gotten involved in some HR-related groups. I forget the name of the committee, but this group was a cross-section of employees in the organization. We talked about company culture and discussed ways to infuse the Fish! philosophy at work. It was created by John Christensen and modeled after the Pike Place Fish Market, to improve organizational culture. It had four components: Choose your attitude, play, make someone's day and be there. The focus of our meetings was to come up with ways to engage the stores in these different ways. I remember we had consultants come in to conduct engagement surveys and focus groups. This work brought me back to my organizational behavior days at Boston College. I got permission to chat with one consultant—because I was still working under the premise of asking for permission vs. asking for forgiveness—and out of that conversation and others I had after that, I decided to go back to school and pursue studies in industrial-organizational psychology.

Once again, it felt great to start anew. To begin a new chapter, learn something of interest, something that mattered. My colorful career path had, up to that point, included temping at different companies; working in retail; working for a beverage company; working at a university; working at an HR consulting group. I was curious about corporate culture, working in groups and leadership. I have always found organizational and human behavior quite fascinating, ever since I was a child. We don't quite leave our childhoods at the door, just because we work in a company. That's my observation anyway.

I went to The California School of Professional Psychology at Alliant International University. I met yet another wonderful group of individuals and professors, some of whom I consider to be good friends to this day. This was the first time I really enjoyed school. I loved the subject matter, talking about team dynamics, leadership, organizational change. I enjoyed being around people I could relate to. This was an executive format for working people. These sorts of programs are tailored to accommodate a schedule such as the one I juggled, between working full time and wanting to continue my education. Of all the classes I took, I fell in love with the area of coaching. I think it was because I was so interested in my development as a human being. It makes sense, right?

I even did a coaching program with CTI (The Coaches Training Institute). I became involved with a wonderful SoCal group called the Professional Coaches and Mentors Association (PCMA).

I graduated from California School of Professional Psychology at Alliant International University with a PsyD in organizational development. I began working in the health care industry doing the thing I love to do as much as art, which is coaching and helping others develop with their leadership. At the time of this writing, I've been in the organization for almost 10 years. It's been a wonderful journey, and I'm just about on the usual spot on my timeline, where I feel ripe for "re-potting."

Today

Once again, I'm asking myself, what's next? It's only been in the last two or three years that I started painting and exhibiting again. And how can I merge my two talents of art and coaching? This is where I am today.

PAINTING YOUR PATH

As I mentioned at the beginning, the original intention for this book was simply to share inspiring stories of women over 40 who were not international celebrities. After doing the interviews and rereading their stories, I couldn't help but notice a few themes, while also taking inventory of my life experiences.

I decided to write this section in case anyone reading this book is in transition and wondering: What about me? What's my next chapter in life? How can I go from being inspired to taking action? I didn't want to leave anyone hanging.

Here are some reflective questions to ponder and some suggestions on what you can do next. I wanted to keep it simple so you could do a little planning and, more importantly, be in action.

Dream

I believe that many of us have something inside us that we secretly wish we could do in life, do "for real." Whether it's something that we view as a hobby, just for fun, or a possible career change or maybe it's a side hustle. Something that brings us joy is a service to others, and maybe it brings in an income. For me, it was a constant voice that said, "People have always gone to you for advice, to listen, what's that about? You're an artist. Create."

Action Time: Do you have a little voice inside your head that keeps encouraging you to do something? I call that little voice intuition. Hint: The message doesn't go away until you do something about it. Not sure?

Try This: Go to a place where you can be by yourself. Maybe it's a guest room or a closet, or maybe you have to get out of the house and check into a hotel for an evening. I know people who have done this! Get quiet. No distractions. No cellphone. Take a moment to close your eyes. Ask yourself, is there something I've always wanted to try? Listen for the answer. Write it down.

No Answer? Try This: Go back through your life and career. What are you known for among your friends, family, co-workers? Ask them. What common theme(s) did you hear? Write it all down.
Still No Answer? Try This: Take this online personality assessment: http://www.humanmetrics.com/cgi-win/jtypes2.asp and see what comes up.

Decide

Once you've spent a little bit of time dreaming, it's time to decide. You have a list of ideas you could move forward with, and you cannot do everything at once. Go back through the list and ask yourself which one thing excites you the most. What would you choose if you knew you couldn't fail? Assume that success is inevitable.

"Decision is the ultimate power." That quote was attributed to Tony Robbins, motivational speaker and author. Once you have an idea of where you want to go next with your life and your career, decide you will pursue it. Name it. Say it out loud. Many of the women in the book hit a wall where staying where they were was no longer an option.

Action Time: What is the one thing you want to pursue next? Too many ideas?

Try This: Assume all of these ideas are billion-dollar ideas. Don't question, just try this on. All of them will be a huge success. Success is inevitable. Which idea are you most inspired and excited by? Circle that idea. Start there. Don't overthink.

Create a Plan

Author Antoine de Saint-Exupéry said, "A goal without a plan is just a wish." You have your idea. Now it's time to plan out how you're going to reach this goal or see this idea to fruition. Again, don't overthink it.

Action Time: What is one thing you could do today, this week, this month, in the next 90 days in your new direction? Write it down. Map it out. What milestones do you want to reach? Not sure what to do?

Try This: If you're stuck, not sure how to go about your plan, reach out to a friend or family member who has been where you want to go. Do some searching on Facebook. There are groups that you can reach out to with questions.

Be Brave—Be in Action

A common phrase my interviewees used is take a risk. You are embarking on your journey. Some friends, family, significant others might not understand what you're up to, and that is A-OK. Believe in yourself. As Thoreau said, "Go confidently in the direction of your dreams. Live a life you've imagined."

Action Time: Take out your plan and work your plan. Do the thing you're most scared to do. Make the phone call. Send out the email. Take the camera off the shelf and start taking photographs. Open up the Word document and start typing. Start that YouTube channel. Whatever your idea is, get to work.

Self-Care

Breaking out of your comfort zone can take effort and energy out of you. Make time to nourish yourself. Meditate for a few minutes a day. There are so many helpful videos out there on YouTube. There are apps like Calm, Insight Timer, and Haven. Work on your mindset.

Try This: Spend a few minutes on conscious breathing. Take three slow inhales. Let your belly expand on the inhale. Hold your breath for three seconds and then slowly exhale for three. Repeat for as many cycles as needed.

Assess

I've learned that if we give ourselves too much time, we don't get important things done. We are only on this planet for a finite amount of time. Set 90-day goals. I've learned this from online mentors like James Wedmore and Todd Herman.

Action Time: As you did in the previous section, you created goals. Now it's time to look back and ask yourself, did I achieve my milestone? What worked? What didn't work?

Try This: Write it out. Did you achieve what you set to achieve in the past 90 days—yes or no? Did you have a specific money goal you wanted to hit over the past 90 days? Did you achieve it—yes or no?

Celebrate Wins

We are so quick to look at the negative. It's critical to identify your progress.

Action Time: On a daily basis, journal at least one positive action you took moving toward your goal(s). You decide what the win is.

I hope this was helpful. If you need additional support, don't hesitate to reach out. I'm here for you.
You can find me at the following places:

@ccr_sunshine
www.clarissastudio.com/
email: clarissa@clarissastudio.com
linkedin.com/in/ccastilloramsey

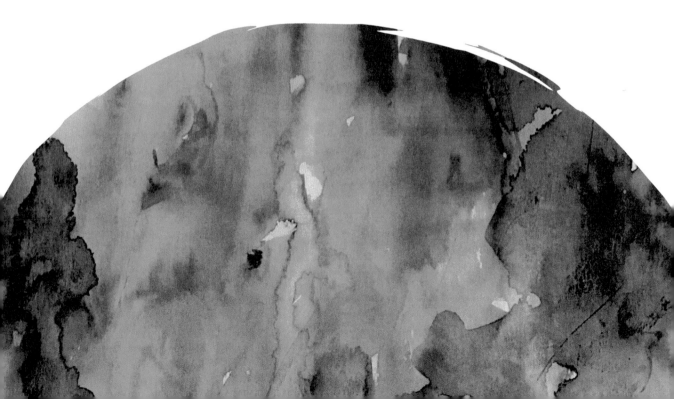

Keep doing you! I wish you all the best!

I am so filled with gratitude to everyone who made this book become a reality. It really does take a village, as they say. There are many people I would like to acknowledge and thank.

A heartfelt thank-you to kn literary arts and my editor, Sarah Bossenbroek. Her thoughtful questions helped me to dig deeper during this process. I appreciate your insight and perspective. Jason Buchholz, who was my first contact at kn literary arts, thank-you for your patience with all my questions and for connecting me to Sarah. A huge thank you to Amazon/KDP for your platform so I could publish this book. Thank you to Diana Adaros, my graphics guru, for putting this book together.

Special thanks go to my friends for your encouragement and support throughout this process. A warm shout out to my DKYDJ mastermind. I appreciate the accountability! To my online mentors and community, thank you for the inspiration: Cathy Heller, Ann Rea, Jonathan Fields, James Wedmore, Ashley Longshore, Selena Soo, Todd Herman, Marie Forleo, Liz Gilbert, Jen Sincero, Dr. Joe Dispenza, Jenna Kutcher, Simon Sinek, Marshall Goldsmith, Lisa Congdon, Julia Cameron and Jasmine Star. Thank you to my husband Robbie (my devil's advocate), for always being there for me. You continue to push me to expand past my perceived limitations. We all need that someone who keeps us moving forward.

The biggest thank-you goes to all the women I interviewed for this book. Your stories are inspiring to me, and each one is a study in what's possible. I'm excited to share your stories with the world. Thank you for being courageous and sharing your stories with me. I know you will inspire other women out there to do their thing, keep growing, and living their best lives. As I like to say, "You do you!" ■